ARTICLES OF FAITH

OXFORD
UNIVERSITY PRESS

Oxford University Press, Inc., publishes works that further
Oxford University's objective of excellence
in research, scholarship, and education.

Oxford   New York
Auckland   Cape Town   Dar es Salaam   Hong Kong   Karachi
Kuala Lumpur   Madrid   Melbourne   Mexico City   Nairobi
New Delhi   Shanghai   Taipei   Toronto

With offices in
Argentina   Austria   Brazil   Chile   Czech Republic   France   Greece
Guatemala   Hungary   Italy   Japan Poland   Portugal   Singapore
South Korea   Switzerland   Thailand   Turkey   Ukraine   Vietnam

Copyright (c) 1936, 1937, 1938, 1951, 1954, 1978, 1980, 1981, 1987 Verdant
This edition (c) 2006 Verdant
Introduction, notes and "Our Man in Tallinn" (c) 2006 Ian Thomson

Published by Oxford University Press, Inc.
198 Madison Avenue, New York, New York 10016
www.oup.com

First published by Signal Books, Ltd. in the United Kingdom.

Oxford is a registered trademark of Oxford University Press

Library of Congress cataloging-in-publication data is available.

ISBN-13: 978-0-19-531499-1 (cloth: alk. paper)
ISBN-10: 0-19-531499-9 (cloth: alk. paper)

1 3 5 7 9 8 6 4 2

Cover Design: Baseline Arts
Cover Image courtesy *The Tablet*
Art & Production: Devdan Sen

Printed in India

ARTICLES OF FAITH

THE COLLECTED *TABLET* JOURNALISM
OF
GRAHAM GREENE

Edited with an introduction by Ian Thomson

OXFORD
UNIVERSITY PRESS

2006

Contents

Contents

ILLUSTRATIONS

Every effort has been made to obtain the necessary permissions with reference to copyright material. The publishers apologize if inadvertently any source remains unacknowledged.

INTRODUCTION

In 1939 Graham Greene wrote to his brother Hugh: "A new shade for knickers and nightdresses has been named Brighton Rock by Peter Jones", adding: "Is this fame?" Greene was then thirty-five: *Brighton Rock* (1938) was his first critically acclaimed religious novel. It describes a betrayal of loyalties in gangland Britain and remains a disquieting parable of conscience. Greene had converted to Catholicism thirteen years earlier. In his three subsequent theological novels—*The Power and the Glory* (1940), *The Heart of the Matter* (1948), *The End of the Affair* (1951)—his gift was to locate the moment of crisis when a character loses faith, religious or otherwise, and life is exposed in all its drab wonder. By the time of his death in 1991, Greene had more than thirty novels to his name: he was a prolific chronicler of wretchedness and damaged faith.

All his life, Greene exercised a judicious censorship over his work and made no secret of his reluctance to appoint a biographer. His "authorized biographer", the now legendary Norman Sherry, devoted thirty years to his reclusive subject. Sherry's first, 700-page volume, published in 1989, scrutinized Greene's every depression, love affair and alcoholic spree. "Oh why does Sherry waste so much time talking about me?" Greene grumbled, though he was probably amused by his chronicler's dedication to the task. [1]

After Greene died at the age of 86, more biographies followed. In competition with Sherry, the American academic Michael Shelden offered a life study, *Graham Greene: The Enemy Within* (1994), which sought to expose a darker shade of Greene. Shelden went to great lengths to arraign his subject on charges of sadism, anti-Semitism and alcoholism. Reportedly Greene had indulged in heterosexual buggery in Jamaica ("Such disgusting sheets") and enjoyed the frisson of adulterous copulation behind Italian church altars. If that was not enough, Greene was accused of complicity in a gruesome 1930s Brighton murder (to this day unsolved) of a pregnant woman whose dismembered body was found in two suitcases. Shelden also insinuates that Greene was essentially homosexual. However, he was not the only biographer to challenge Sherry's monopoly.

In the race to commemorate Greene, a third man appeared: Anthony Mockler. Mockler's *Graham Greene: Three Lives* came out in 1994. The cover proclaimed: "Novelist! Explorer! Spy!" and the author's description of Greene on his Swiss deathbed was accordingly *Boy's Own* in tone: "Graham looked out of the antiseptic room over the sterile Swiss sky. No vultures gazed back..." Clearly the shabby world of Greene's fiction had exerted a spell. The Catholic priest who administered the last rites to Greene in Switzerland, Father Leopoldo Durán, confessed to rummaging through the writer's waste-paper basket in search of revealing letters: his memoir, *Graham Greene: Friend and Brother* (1994), was distinguished by an excess of devotion.

Greene's fallible, ambivalent characters are unlike any in British fiction. Pinkie, the juvenile hoodlum of *Brighton Rock*, murders without a qualm, yet, as a lapsed Catholic, he fears damnation, and Greene establishes our empathy for him. In Catholicism Greene had found a sense of melodrama—an atmosphere of good and evil—that was useful to him as a novelist. Over the sixty years of his writing career he created characters who try to hide their weaknesses from the world and themselves. Few novelists have fathomed with such intensity the suffering of this earth. In Catholic terms, Greene was a moralist excited by human turpitude and evil in our times.

Not surprisingly, the unsparing bleakness of Greene's vision has influenced a number of contemporary novelists, among them John le Carré, Muriel Spark and the Belfast-born Brian Moore. However, Greene remains inimitable: when Philip Larkin tried to parody the author of *The Heart of the Matter* in a weekly magazine, the result was memorably awful: 'Hatred moved in him like fatigue as, unsurprised, he recognised betrayal." Although Greene claimed to dislike the label "Catholic novelist", he retained his faith, if not his *belief*, in Catholicism all his life. To his dying day indeed he kept a photograph in his wallet of the Italian stigmatic Padre Pio, whose hands and feet were said to display the wounds of Christ. Whether these lesions were of neurotic origin—psychological rather than supernatural—Greene did not care to know: he wanted there to be a mystery at the heart of life. It may seem incredible that an intelligent man could be awed by the irrationality of stigmatism. But, as Greene told *The Tablet* in 1989:

"There *is* a mystery. There is something inexplicable in human life."

Over a period of fifty years, the British Catholic weekly *The Tablet* provided Greene with a forum for both his works-in-progress and his frequently unorthodox religious views. A writer of religious doubt rather than of religious certainty, Greene was less interested in the rituals and practice of Catholicism than in the moral questions it raised. His reportage, book reviews and essays for *The Tablet* reflect this interest. Much of the material has not been seen since the 1930s and is collected here for the first time. As well as offering a companion to Professor Sherry, *Articles of Faith* illuminates the pleasures, foibles and eccentric dislikes of Greene. The collection moreover confirms the novelist's considerable wit, capacity for terse put-downs and fascination for what remained outside his class and culture—whether it was blue films in post-Franco Spain or Catholic churches in Indo-China. Above all, *Articles of Faith* records a religious faith that endured.

✳   ✳   ✳

Greene first contributed to *The Tablet* in 1936 when he was living in London with his wife Vivien Dayrell-Browning, who was expecting their second child. *Brighton Rock* was progressing by fits and starts; Greene was also busy with his journalism. As well as writing film reviews for *The Spectator*, he was subsequently literary editor of *Night and Day*, a *New Yorker*-style magazine which lasted for just six months of 1937. Greene had married Vivien, a committed Catholic, in 1927, having converted to Rome a year earlier. By introducing Greene to Catholic Christianity, Vivien changed the course of her husband's life and enabled him to become the writer we admire today. In later years, however, she claimed that Greene defected to Rome because he was intellectually convinced by Catholicism, not merely to please her.

It seemed that Greene grappled with this argument all his life. John Cornwell's celebrated interview with the novelist for *The Tablet* in 1989 ("Why I am still a Catholic") suggests an eighty-five-year-old who was troubled by theological doubts but still dogged by the possibility of God. Many ambiguities emerge from the interview. For example,

Greene claims to be agnostic yet he occasionally attends Mass. In old age he was reluctant to take Communion and did not like to go to confession: frequent lapses into lust and adultery had prevented him from leading a virtuous Catholic life. (Revealingly, Greene tells Cornwell that he dislikes the word "sin": he did not feel himself to be in a state of grace.) Greene's soured Catholic faith was never more amply expressed than in *The Tablet* interview; I have included it here.

✳   ✳   ✳

In the 1930s *The Tablet* offices were in the City of London at 39 Paternoster Row (later destroyed in a Luftwaffe raid). The editor was the portly Douglas Woodruff, an acquaintance of Evelyn Waugh and Hilaire Belloc. Under Woodruff's urbane editorship *The Tablet* became less "churchy" and began to reach out to the laity. By instinct, tradition and education, however, Woodruff was a conservative; like Belloc, he was favourable to Franco's Catholic cause in Spain and was attracted to the thorny asceticism of Spanish Catholicism. A "Red scare" had spread across Europe in the wake of the 1917 Bolshevik Revolution, and Woodruff was among a generation of younger Anglo-Catholics who were seeking an alternative to atheist Communism. In Spain the leftist government that preceded Franco's had been virulently and crudely anti-religious; the persecution and slaughter of Spanish priests was roundly condemned by Evelyn Waugh and others in *The Tablet* circle.

Though Greene did not know him until later, the most influential of *The Tablet*'s associates in the 1930s was Father Martin D'Arcy, SJ, a charismatic if faintly snobbish figure bent on casuitical "persuasion" and the conversion of Anglicans to Rome. Greene met D'Arcy twenty years after he had been received into the Catholic Church and was not an enthusiastic admirer. ("I don't believe that any priest ever converts anyone", he tartly remarked of D'Arcy.) [2] Indeed, while Greene's 1930s *Tablet* journalism dutifully scorns Communism, neither did it endorse D'Arcy's or Woodruff's Francoist sympathies; Greene was declaredly anti-Fascist.

Politically, Greene's position at *The Tablet* was thus somewhat

Douglas Woodruff, editor of *The Tablet* (1936-67) when Graham Greene first wrote for the journal.

awkward. In the received notion, any Englishman who was openly anti-Fascist in the 1930s was assumed to be *anti*-Catholic and for the Spanish Republic. Yet Greene was a Catholic—and a leftist. Whose side was he on? Not surprisingly these conflicting loyalties and shifting political allegiances would colour Greene's novels. The Spanish Civil War may even have reflected a personal anxiety of Greene's. His father had been the pious Anglican headmaster of a public school in Berkhamsted near London; Graham experienced divided loyalties each day as he left the family quarters to go to class. Frontiers (whether geographical, religious or political) have a dynamism of their own in Greene's fiction and set off a reflex of unease.

At first Greene reviewed for *The Tablet*'s "Fiction Chronicle", and was given free rein to choose what novels he liked. Broad-minded, he praised Stevie Smith's first fiction, *Novel on Yellow Paper* (so named after the yellow paper on which the novel was typed), as well as Djuna Barnes' extravagantly baroque novella *Nightwood*, which was ignored by the British quality newspapers and Sunday broadsheets. Though occasionally wordy, Greene was a lucid critic for *The Tablet*, fiercely set against the nebulous or abstruse; any author he considered to be pretentious or self-indulgent was neatly tossed and gored. John van Druten, the playwright and novelist, caters for "lonely middle-class ladies with artistic interests", while the multifarious Eric Linklater is upbraided for his Rabelaisian excess ("Words, words, words"). The notion that literary style is a decoration—something you can apply to your subject—never appealed to Greene.

Some of Greene's literary judgements are perplexing. The American novelist John Dos Passos is dismissed as a "heavy-handed Socialist Galsworthy", yet his leftist support of Republican Spain and the Joycean experimentation of his fiction impressed Greene. (Indeed, he said as much on accepting the John Dos Passos Prize for literature in 1980.) Another surprising target of Greene is the St. Petersburg-born novelist William Gerhardie. The author of *Futility* and *The Polyglots* has "great talent", Greene concedes, "but he never quite achieves anything completely memorable". In his private correspondence, however, Greene expresses an admiration for Gerhardie; whether he had patronized him in *The Tablet* from a contrary whim or a stubborn streak is unclear.

For all its vinegary humour, Greene's *Tablet* journalism imparts a lively sense of involvement in the politics and literature of the time. During the mid-1930s Greene made a trip to the Estonian capital of Tallinn; there he got to know a British diplomat, Peter Leslie, who was also a Catholic convert and apparently involved in espionage. (The Greene-Leslie correspondence is the subject of my article, "Our Man in Tallinn", which closes *Articles of Faith*.) An habitué of shadowy places, Greene was the only Catholic writer in Britain to recommend Ignazio Silone's Italian novel, *Bread and Wine*. As the title suggests, the novel is fraught with the symbols of the bread and wine of the Eucharist, and moreover carries a Christian Socialist message of redemption for Italy's poor. By the time *Bread and Wine* reached its first readers in 1937, Mussolini had conquered Abyssinia (now Ethiopia) and further allied the Fascist State to the Catholic Church. To the Catholic orthodoxy Silone was a left-wing propagandist [3], but Greene defended Silone's attempts to reconcile Catholicism with Socialism: "His criticism is not hasty, shallow or partisan", but "profoundly Christian". On the whole, Greene was at pains to champion anti-Fascist writers like Silone who advocated "social justice". (It is unlikely, however, that he knew of Silone's alleged espionage activities, which involved Greenian elements of treachery and double-dealing.) [4]

Many other authors under Greene's review are now forgotten. John Masefield, a former Poet Laureate, is scarcely read today. Arthur Calder-Marshall is also unfortunately neglected. Other literary aspirants whom Greene praised in *The Tablet*, though, have endured. R. K. Narayan, the South Indian novelist, benefited greatly from Greene's advocacy of his work in *The Tablet* and elsewhere. (Greene even advised the author on what pen-name to use and moreover saw to his financial security.) Greene's correspondence with Narayan runs to some 140 letters and covers half a century. [5]

Whenever Greene was at *The Tablet* he made a point of visiting Tom Burns. Two years younger than Greene, Burns was a junior director of the Catholic newspaper and a publisher with Longmans. The Jesuit-educated Burns, a cradle Catholic, was outwardly very different from the theologically troubled Greene and certainly did not share his taste for brothels. ("Let's go to Limehouse tonight, there's a ballet of Chinese nudes at the local theatre!" Greene once suggested to Burns.) They first met in 1929 after Greene had completed his third (but first to be published) novel, *The Man Within*. To Burns the twenty-four-year-old Greene seemed "witty, evasive, nervous, sardonic"; nevertheless Burns remarked on the "serenity" of the novelist's Queen Anne house in Clapham. No doubt this air of calm was due to Vivien Greene's homemaking, as Greene was not interested in domesticity. Unknown to Vivien, indeed, he had begun to frequent prostitutes. Burns' personal memoir of Greene, first published in *The Tablet* in 1991, appears in *Articles of Faith*.

Over drinks one evening, Greene told Burns of his plan to write a book about the recent persecution of the Mexican church under President Plutarco Calles and the Cristero peasant revolt it provoked.

Tom Burns, editor of *The Tablet* (1967-82), and his wife Mabél with Pope John Paul II in Rome in 1980.

Calles had ordered the most pitiless clamp-down on Catholicism anywhere "since Queen Elizabeth I", said Greene. Cristero rebels had marched courageously under the banner of Our Lady of Guadalupe to demand that their churches be re-opened; by 1927 most of the leaders were defeated, captured or executed. In Mexico (where some 50,000 Cristeros had died during the neo-Stalinist purge of Catholicism) Greene was to catch a glimpse of what the world might be like without religion. Evelyn Waugh's 1935 biography of the Catholic martyr Edmund Campion had already deeply moved him. In Waugh's tale of heroism and holiness in Tudor England, Greene found parallels between Campion's fate and the fate of Father Pro and the other priests martyred in revolutionary Mexico. Waugh's biography, not surprisingly, was written with the help of Douglas Woodruff; it is a work of sturdy, recusant piety.

The Catholic publishers most likely to back Greene, Sheed & Ward, were wary. Mexico was too far away and it was feared that Greene's book would lose its relevance if the persecutions were to cease entirely. In early December 1937 Greene therefore made a tentative approach to Longmans through Tom Burns. "Burns would be quite ready, I think, to take over the English rights from Sheed if it can be arranged", Greene wrote to his London agent. He added: "Personally, I would much rather be published by Longmans—it would brand one less in the public eye as a Catholic writer." Eventually, thanks to Burns, Longmans commissioned Greene's book: *The Position of the Church in Mexico* (as it was originally and rather blandly entitled) went for £500, an appreciable sum in those days.

The man Evelyn Waugh nicknamed "Grisjambon Vert" (Graham Greene) left London for Mexico on 29 January 1938. He was thirty-three and his career prospects looked dismal after *Night and Day* had been forced to close down the previous month due to a lawsuit. (Twentieth Century Fox had issued libel proceedings against Greene for his "defamatory" remarks about Shirley Temple in her film *Wee Willie Winkie*; the child-star exuded a "dimpled depravity", Greene wrote in *Night and Day*, that would appeal to elderly clergymen.) To top it all, Greene's son Francis had recently been born, and his birth filled the novelist with anxious expectation for the future. By the time Greene arrived in Mexico the worst of the persecutions were in fact over. However, the evidence lingered in the burned churches, the smashed effigies of saints, and in the ridicule of priests in broadsheets and burlesques.

The five weeks which Greene spent in Mexico resulted in *The Lawless Roads* (1939), an exceptionally bleak and dyspeptic travel book. Portions of it first appeared in *The Tablet*; they are republished here. Oddly, while journalists are the most heinous characters in Greene's fiction (think of the mannish Mabel Warren in *Stamboul Train*, or the cynical Montagu Parkinson in *A Burnt-Out Case*), Greene was a superb reporter. The controlled understatement and unsparing lucidity of his Mexican reportage unforgettably portrays the aftermath of the violent "revolution" [6] begun by President Calles: churches stand shuttered in the "mosquito-noisy air"; buzzards have "tiny moron" heads.

Though Greene's Catholicism had surely wavered since his conversion, in Mexico it was strengthened. The novel that emerged from his Mexican travels, *The Power and the Glory* (1940), investigates the operation of divine grace through one man's brokenness and despair. The book's whisky priest moreover provides a symbolic re-enactment of Campion's martyrdom four centuries earlier; all the blood, hatred and derision of 1920s Mexico are visited on Greene's fugitive priest. In the priest's alcoholic journey towards martyrdom, however, the Vatican suspected an attempt by Greene to denigrate orthodox Catholicism. (This would not be the first time that Greene, a provoking and paradoxical writer, incurred pontifical displeasure.)

When Greene returned to England in May 1938 the country was preparing for war. Body bags, buckets of fire-fighting sand, and generators were put on standby. Following the declaration of war on 3 September 1939, Vivien Greene took her two children to Crowborough to stay with her parents-in-law, and afterwards to the safety of Trinity College, Oxford. (Greene had originally intended that they decamp to Jamaica.) Greene stayed on in London, where his life was about to change. In 1940, during one of his infrequent visits to Oxford, he told Vivien that a landmine had destroyed their Clapham house. At the time Greene was living in secret with another woman and so escaped harm ("Graham's life was saved by his infidelity," Vivien later acidly remarked). On visiting the house at 14 North Side, Clapham Common, Greene's wife found that most of the Queen Anne furniture had been stolen and her photographs, diaries and letters destroyed. Greene would describe such scenes of rubble in his 1942 novel of London during the Blitz, *The Ministry of Fear*, life, as it often did for Greene, was imitating art.

For eight months Greene worked with Tom Burns at the Ministry of Information (the British equivalent of Germany's Propaganda Ministry). Always interested, Burns suggested that Greene write the life of Father Damien, the Belgian leper colony priest who died from the disease. Nothing came of the idea. Instead Greene contemplated a biography of the Victorian explorer Henry Morton Stanley. (The book, provisionally entitled *The Rear Column: An African Mystery*, was also abandoned—owing to a rival Stanley biographer.) What to do? In 1941, Greene was posted to West Africa on behalf of the SIS, more commonly known as MI6. He was stationed in Sierra Leone until 1944, when he returned to London to work under Kim Philby.

As the 1940s gave way to the 1950s, Greene's contact with Douglas Woodruff diminished; theirs was anyway an incongruous relationship, based on a hatred of Communism (which Greene did not always share) and a love of G. K. Chesterton's Father Brown and Victorian mystery tales.[7] Under Woodruff's guidance, however, Greene was persuaded to publish in *The Tablet* his extraordinary essay on Catholic devotion to Mary and Marian apparitions. "Our Lady and Her Assumption" had first appeared in *Life* magazine in 1951, six years after the war's end. Accordingly, the essay is touched by the holocaust of Hiroshima and the brutality of Stalin's technocratic Russia. "Today the human body is regarded as expendable material, something to be eliminated wholesale by the atom bomb, a kind of anonymous carrion."[8] If Greene's determination to spot God beneath the banalities of everyday life feels occasionally contrived, his essay on the Assumption reveals a man of lingering and, I think, instinctive piety. It is republished in *Articles of Faith*.

Indo-China, more so than 1930s Mexico, brought Greene face-to-face with physical danger and the feelings of exhilaration he claimed to crave. (An American friend of Greene's in Saigon believed the novelist wanted to be "crucified on an anthill in a third world country".) Greene first visited south-east Asia in the early 1950s for the beauty, he said, of its women. Vietnam was then in a state of civil war. The colonial French were being ousted by the Communist Viet Minh, and France's post-war rule in the region was coming to an end. An extract from Greene's Indo-China journal, "Catholics at War", appeared in *The Tablet* in 1954. In it, Greene relates how his jeep stopped short of a land-mine; he and his driver escaped death, yet Greene takes his reprieve ungraciously: "It is too difficult to thank God with any sincerity for this gift of life." For Greene, the thrill of travel on the dangerous edge was perhaps a way out of depression, or simply a means to escape boredom. Some of his personal observations in "Catholics at War" later found their way into *The Quiet American* (1955), Greene's greatest political novel, set in Vietnam. I have included the journal excerpt here.

✳ ✳ ✳

By 1947 Greene had announced to his wife that he no longer loved her; he was involved with a married American, Catherine Walston. In her husband's absence, Vivien cultivated an interest in antique dolls' houses. It seemed that she found comfort in the miniature world of these houses since her own home—14 North Side—had been destroyed by fire. Euan Cameron visited Vivien some time in the late 1980s as he hoped to publish a book on her collection. Cameron had been a director of Greene's publishers, The Bodley Head, and knew Greene personally. Before he left, Vivien took him on a tour of her Oxfordshire house. Cameron recalled: "On entering one of the bedrooms, she announced to me: 'This is Graham's room.' I was amazed, for I knew they had not lived together for over forty years. There, on a pillow, with the crisply ironed linen sheet turned back, was a pair of men's pyjamas. 'They're ready for when Graham comes home,' said Vivien, as she turned away to continue our tour." [9] Marriage was an indissoluble sacrament for the devout Vivien, who referred to herself as "Mrs Graham Greene" until her death in 2003.

The last of Greene's companions, Yvonne Cloetta, was with him when he died and is mentioned in the novelist's letters to Tom Burns. Greene first met Cloetta on a visit to French Cameroon in 1959, when his love for Catherine Walston was waning. Cloetta was then married to a wealthy businessman based in Africa and, by her own account, bored. The meeting seems to have been a classic *coup de foudre*. Cloetta, stylish, blonde, petite, captivated Greene and, in a decorous way, he began to court her. At fifty-five, Greene was twenty years older than Cloetta, unhappily married to Vivien, and, he felt, on the ebb-tide of his achievements. His greatest work—the "Catholic" novels—was behind him.

Yet Cloetta was able to ease the writer through his brooding introspection, and became his lifelong counsellor and confidante. She oversaw French translations of Greene's books, suggested titles for them and even edited the journal he kept of his dreams, *A World of My Own*, published posthumously in 1992. Cloetta was effectively Greene's *de facto* spouse; indeed he was furious when she was described in the 1989 *Tablet* interview as his "girlfriend". ("How could I possibly refer to somebody I have known for thirty years as a girlfriend?" Greene complained to Tom Burns. "I think I must have thought the interview was over and we were talking vaguely but not as vaguely as that.")

In 1966 Greene moved to France to be near Cloetta, who was then living in the Midi with her husband. From his fourth-floor flat overlooking Antibes harbour Greene maintained a spirited correspondence with *The Tablet*. In his twenty-odd letters to the paper he attacked Pope John Paul II, Ronald Reagan, Archbishop Marcinkus, as well as the dictators Pinochet and Jean-Claude ("Baby Doc") Duvalier. Christopher Hawtree's diverting collection of Greene's letters to the press, *Yours Etc*, reveals a man with a gift to subvert; by raising two fingers at what passed for the establishment, Greene enlivened newspaper correspondence columns.

At the age of seventy-one, in 1976, Greene was appointed a Trustee of *The Tablet* Trust headed by the Duke of Norfolk. At first he demurred as he did not want any financial involvement. "I hadn't realised that the Trustees would hold at any rate some nominal shares in *The Tablet* and this disquiets me", Greene wrote to Burns. "It is out of the question for me to hold any shares in England as I am domiciled abroad, so I think that at the next meeting you should offer my regretful resignation as Trustee." However, Greene was reluctant to disappoint an old friend, and remained on the board.

Burns had taken over in 1967 from Douglas Woodruff as editor of *The Tablet*. For thirty-one years the Catholic paper had been "D.W.'s Weekly", but the world was now a different place. Woodruff's vision of the Holy See as conservative and hierarchical had failed to represent the emergent new Church following the 1962-1965 Vatican II reforms. In 1963 (no doubt to Greene's approval) the beaming Pope John XXIII had published his famous encyclical *Pacem in Terris* ("Peace on Earth"), which opened up a dialogue between the Catholic and Marxist worlds. Europe was changing, and Burns wanted *The Tablet* to catch the new mood. He had spent much of the Second World War as press attaché to the British embassy in Madrid, and, unlike Woodruff, was not uncritical of Franco. Under his fifteen-year editorship until 1982 *The Tablet* was transformed into the Catholic equivalent of *The Guardian* or *The Observer*, open to divergent theological and political views.

Greene's correspondence with Burns radiates an impish mischief and candour; yet it has been ignored by the novelist's several biographers and all academics. Greene provided Burns with ideas to enliven *The Tablet*. He proposed Lord Longford, the philosopher Freddie Ayer and the novelist Piers Paul Reid as candidates for a *Tablet* questionnaire on the subject of religious beliefs. ("What do you mean by God?", "Do you pray, and if so, why?") However, Greene thought the paper's literary standards had declined over the years, and he told Burns as much. "Considering how few books of fiction you review it does seem rather a waste of space to give up anything to enthusiastic reviews of Morris West... If to be widely read is a criterion for being reviewed in *The Tablet*, then I think the sooner I cease to be a Trustee the better."

Shortly before Christmas 1978, nevertheless, Greene submitted to *The Tablet* an unfinished story about a priest called Father

Quixote. The fragment was inspired by the boozy motoring excursions which Greene had enjoyed over the years in Spain with Father Leopoldo Durán (the model for his fictional Quixote). Bottles of Galician wine were stowed in their car as the men checked into monasteries and hostels. (Perhaps Greene had wanted to turn Durán into a whisky priest: Durán was often squiffy from tots of Cutty Sark.) Burns was delighted with the story, and asked Greene to write further episodes in the fortunes of the Spanish padre. Greene hesitated: Father Quixote was quite different from the alcoholic, fear-ridden priest of *The Power and the Glory*, and he could not see how his character might be developed. After an interval, however, Greene offered two more stories, by which time Father Quixote had acquired a personality of his own. The novel which became *Monsignor Quixote* (1982) was thus born in the pages of *The Tablet*. All three fragments are included in *Articles of Faith*, though they differ very slightly from the finished book. (Father Quixote's Italian "Fiat Five" was altered to the Spanish "Seat 600"; a bottle of Italian "Marsala", similarly, became "malaga".) Those unfamiliar with *Monsignor Quixote* will be entertained by the stories; they are worth re-reading anyway.

Throughout the 1970s Greene continued to take an interest in *The Tablet*. With his customary generosity he offered Burns a selection of his own manuscripts for a *Tablet* fund-raising sale at Sotheby's in 1979. One of these, *One Hundred and Ten Airports*, was the first volume of Greene's autobiography, subsequently re-titled *A Sort of Life*. Greene also sent Burns the typescript for a "new play", *For Whom the Bell Chimes* (to this day unperformed), along with his introduction written in 1936 or 1937 to R. K. Narayan's second novel, *Bachelor of Arts*. In the course of their sixty-year friendship, Greene and Burns were tactful with each other, and Burns was quick to commiserate with Greene when his friend Omar Torrijos, the Panamanian military leader, died in August 1981. Greene had revered Torrijos for his struggle to disengage from American control. "Torrijos is one of the friends whom I miss most now that he is not there", he explained to Burns. "A great man in a tiny country who was having a big influence and yet remained completely human. We had fun together and

Punch cartoon of Graham Greene to mark publication in 1982 of *Monsignor Quixote*. The limerick caption reads:

"The crankiest Christian that ever was seen
Is surely His Eminence Graham Greene.
His creatures find scandal and degradation
The sole sure means to attain salvation".

laughed a lot and he was always ready to help in any way possible."
The kernel of *Getting to Know the General*—Greene's 1984 tribute to
General Torrijos—is contained in that brief letter.

In 1982, on the eve of Burns' retirement from *The Tablet*, the
Falklands War broke out. In a celebrated editorial Burns urged Britain
to desist from Margaret Thatcher's "narrow patriotism" against
Argentina, and Greene found himself in agreement. However, when
Burns asked him to write down what he would say to Pope John Paul
II if he had just five minutes of his time, Greene replied tetchily: "I
think my five minutes with the Pope would only lead to
excommunication!" It was the spring of 1982 and John Paul was
about to visit Britain; Greene disagreed with his intransigent views on
birth control and with much of his politics: "I must say I find the
present Pope intolerable", he went on to Burns. "He has been a
disaster in Central America. A disaster also with his views on
contraception, etc. God knows what he is going to do with poor
Vatican II." Greene's estrangement from John Paul II is the subject of
Alberto Huerta's 1991 *Tablet* essay, "Graham Greene's Way",
reprinted here. In Father Huerta's view, Greene was an advocate of
liberation theology and the leftist Jesuitism now represented in
trouble spots from China to Haiti. ("It is impossible for a Catholic to
remain on the side-lines," he quotes Greene as saying.)

After the papal visit to London in 1982, John Wilkins succeeded
Tom Burns as editor of *The Tablet*. Like Greene, Wilkins was a left-of-
centre convert to the Roman Church, and Greene expressed his
approval of him to Burns: "I am so glad that Wilkins is keeping *The
Tablet* on the liberal lines which you instituted after your very
conservative predecessor" (meaning Douglas Woodruff); he added
affectionately: "*The Tablet* remains a monument to your work."
Greene's final contribution was a poem, "The Grass", published in
1987. The verse is tinged with an autumnal sense of loss and the self-
examination of an old man looking back on his life. Though Greene's
poetry was very slight beside his other work, I include the poem as a
curiosity.

Greene's last known letter to Tom Burns was dated 6 June 1990
after cancer of the blood had been diagnosed: "Forgive a short note

but I have been rather ill and am living in-between blood transfusions." Graham Greene died a year later; a Memorial Requiem Mass was celebrated for him at Westminister Cathedral.

Ian Thomson
London, 2006

NOTES

1 Greene may even have enjoyed the vinous associations of his biographer's surname. "Let's go to Sherry's", a gangster recommends a drinking club in *Brighton Rock*, adding: "I can't stand the place."

2 Letter from Greene to Tom Burns, 28 November 1976.

3 *The Catholic World* (May 1937), for example, dismissed *Bread and Wine* as "a vulgar, pessimistic, bitter and extravagant campaign document aimed at Italian Fascism ... the characters are no more than puppets in a propaganda show."

4 In 1996 it was revealed that roughly from 1919 to 1930 Ignazio Silone had supplied information about his former Communist comrades to a Fascist contact. Silone had been expelled from the Italian Communist Party in 1931 for protesting against the "red Fascism" of its Stalinist members; nevertheless the motivation behind his betrayal (if such it was) remains obscure.

5 On 1 August 1935, Greene wrote to R. K. Narayan: "It is a real joy to be of use to a new writer of your quality", adding a year later: "I feel sure your star is in the ascendant now!" Greene had been worried that the author's real name (Narayan Swami) would hinder sales in Britain. "It's a silly thing to say, but in this country a name which it is difficult for the old ladies in libraries to remember materially affects a book's sales. I saw an excellent novel by a German completely fail because of the supposed

difficulty of his name: Erik von Kuhnelt-Leddihn! But, of course, if R. K. Narayan is absurdly incorrect in Indian eyes, we won't dream of using it."

6   Contrary to the socialist murals of Diego Rivera (with their Soviet-style depiction of a happy Mexican peasantry), Mexico has never known true revolution. The one exception was a brief moment in the mid-1930s when President Lázaro Cardenas bravely confiscated Mexico's petroleum reserves from US Standard Oil. Every subsequent Mexican presidency has been in thrall to America. "Poor Mexico!" runs the famous adage, "so far from God and so close to the United States."

7   See, for example, Douglas Woodruff's *The Tichborne Claimant: A Victorian Mystery* (1957); also, *Victorian Detective Fiction: A Catalogue of the Collection Made by Dorothy Glover and Graham Greene* (1966, Bodley Head).

8   Greene's vision of a world made transient and destructible by technology is echoed in the famous Ferris wheel scene of the film of *The Third Man*, where the Catholic racketeer Harry Lime (Orson Welles) tells his friend Holly Martins: "Nobody thinks in terms of human beings. Governments don't, so why should we?"

9   In 2005, when Euan Cameron asked Graham Greene's daughter Caroline Bourget whether the story had upset her, she said no; nevertheless she preferred to believe that the pyjamas had been laid out for a visiting grandchild.

ACKNOWLEDGEMENTS

Many have helped me to compile *Articles of Faith*; I would like to thank Shelley Barber and Robert O'Neil of the John. J Burns Library (Boston) for their permission to quote from Graham Greene's unpublished letters to Vivien Greene, R. K. Narayan, William Gerhardie, Arthur Calder-Marshall, Tom Burns and Peter Leslie. Jimmy Burns, Tom Burns' son, offered invaluable comments and suggestions. Thanks are also due to: Laura Fleminger, Alberto Huerta, John Cornwell, Adrian Tahourdin, Jeremy Lewis, Austen Ivereigh, Catherine Pepinster, Caroline Lourdas, Lucy Lethbridge, James Ferguson, Michael Walsh (author of *The Tablet: 1840-1990*), Ronan Bennett, Dr. Jan Piggott, Euan Cameron, Amanda Saunders, Richard Greene, Leslie Griffiths and, above all, Miranda France.

✳   ✳   ✳

NOTE ON THE TEXT

Though Graham Greene was unusually attentive to newsprint (he spotted 37 misprints in a single page of the 12 May 1978 edition of *The Listener*) numerous errors appear in his *Tablet* contributions. Where the error is one clearly produced by carelessness, I have corrected it; otherwise I let it stand.

I.T.

REPORTAGE AND COMMENTARY

MEXICAN SUNDAY

Under the dictatorial governor Garrido Canabal, the "swampy and puritanical state" of Tabasco had seen the fiercest anticlericalism in 1920's and 1930's revolutionary Mexico. Canabal, a devotee of President Calles, had terrorized the Cristero rebels, destroyed their churches and chased out every priest. Villahermosa, the Tabascan capital, remained teetotal but Greene had managed to bring with him a bottle of brandy. Canabal had fled to Costa Rica by the time Greene checked into a hotel. ("I was driven to write an article on Tabasco for *The Tablet* while sitting in the Hotel Español", Greene was to record in *The Lawless Roads*.)

"We die like dogs," a woman said to me in Villahermosa. Villahermosa is the capital of Tabasco, ten hours up the shallow, muddy river Grijalva, from the Gulf of Mexico, and Tabasco marks the lowest point to which Catholicism has fallen in Mexico. In most States now, the struggle between Church and State has shifted to the educational field. That, of course, is serious enough: by law, if more than nine people gather together for a religious purpose the house becomes automatically the property of the Government, and a great deal of the religious education in the Federal District is for that reason carried on in half-ruined houses which are not likely to excite the cupidity of an official. In the long run—strategically—the attack on religious education may be worse than an attack on the rites of the Church (one may picture a whole population dropping towards Indian superstition), but as far as immediate human happiness is concerned, I would rather live anywhere than in Tabasco.

Garrido Canabal, the anti-religious fanatic who for so long governed the State, with his organized band of pistoleros called Red Shirts, has gone to Costa Rica, but his work lives. Only one church remains standing in Tabasco, about twenty miles from the capital, and that is now a school. In Villahermosa itself not even a little rubble marks the site of the cathedral—only one of those ugly cement playgrounds with a few grim iron swings which no one seems to use. Of one other church in the capital there does remain a trace—the back wall and a rectangle of broken stones, for the road no one mends. I was told in Mexico City that Garrido, when he passed the law making marriage compulsory for all priests, declared he only wished to legitimize their children. The statement has some value as a wisecrack, but no truth. I talked to Protestants as well as Catholics in Villahermosa, and they all agreed that the priests in Tabasco when Garrido came into power were a fine body of men, better than some in Chiapas and Yucatan, and whenever I inquired if some good had come from the dictatorship in the shape of schools, I was told no—the Church schools were better than anything that exists now.

But Garrido has fled, and yet nothing is done; the Bishop of Campeche is smuggled in by plane to see an old dying woman who can afford the luxury of consolation, but for the poor—they must die like dogs. There are no Masses in private houses as there are in the neighbouring State of Chiapas, only a dreadful lethargy as the Catholics die slowly out—without confession, without the sacraments, the child unbaptized and the dying man unshriven. I thought of Rilke's phrase: "An empty, horrible alley, an alley in a foreign town, in a town where nothing is forgiven."

There are, I suppose, geographical and racial excuses for the lethargy. Tabasco is a State of river and swamp and extreme heat; in northern Chiapas there is no choice between mule and the rare plane for a traveller, and in Tabasco no choice between plane and boat. But a mule is a sociable form of transport—nights spent with strangers huddling together in the cold mountain air, talk over the beans and the embers; while in a boat you are isolated between the banana plantations with the mosquitoes.

And then there are no Indians in Tabasco to shame the Catholic with their wild beliefs and their erroneous, if perverted veneration, into *some* action. Too much foreign blood came into Tabasco when it was a prosperous country: at the end of the American Civil War many Southerners migrated here to trade in mahogany, and stayed. The most common Mexican names in Villahermosa are Graham and Greene. The faith with them goes back only a few generations. They haven't the stability of the old Spanish families in Chiapas.

Nothing in a tropical town can fill the place of a church for the most mundane use: a church is the one spot of coolness out of the vertical sun, a place to sit, a place where the senses can rest a little while from ugliness; it offers to the poor man what a rich man may get in a theatre—though not in Tabasco. Now in Villahermosa, in the blinding heat and the mosquito-noisy air, there is no escape at all for anyone. Garrido did his job well: he knew that the stones cry out, and he didn't leave any stones. There is a kind of cattle-tick you catch in Chiapas, which fastens its head in the flesh: you have to burn it out, otherwise the head remains embedded, and festers. It is an ugly metaphor to use, but an exact one: in northern Chiapas the churches still stand, shuttered and ruined and empty, but they fester—the whole village festers away from the door: the plaza is the first to go.

So in Villahermosa there is nothing to do all the long Sundays that go on and on but sit in Victorian rocking-chairs, swinging back and forth waiting for the sunset and the mosquitoes. The hideous buzzards group themselves on the roofs like pigeons: the tiny moron head, long neck, masked face and dusty plumage, peering this way and that attentively for a death. I counted twenty on one roof. They looked domesticated, as if they were going to lay an egg. And I suppose even a bird of prey does sometimes lay an egg.

Nothing to do but drink gassy fruit drinks (there is prohibition of liquor, too, in Tabasco, and no miracle in the Godless State will turn this aerated water into wine) and watch the horrifying abundance of just life. You can't open a book without some tiny scrap of life scuttling across the page; the stalls are laden with great pulpy, tasteless fruits, and when the lights come out, so do the beetles: the pavement by the green, sour riverside is black with them. You kill them on your bedroom floor, and by morning they have been drained and moved away by more life—the hordes of ants which come up between the tiles at the scent of death.

The anonymity of Sunday seems peculiarly unnatural in Mexico: a man going hunting, a young people's fiesta—nothing else to divide this day from all the other days; no bell to ring. The only place where you can find some symbol of your faith is in the cemetery up on a hill above the town—a great white classical portico and the legend "Silencio," in big black letters, the blind wall round the corner where Garrido shot his prisoners, and inside the enormous tombs of above-ground burial, glass houses for flowers and portraits and images, crosses and weeping angels, the sense of a far better and cleaner city than that of the living at the bottom of the hill.

May 14th, 1938

IN SEARCH OF A MIRACLE

In Chiapas state, bordering on Tabasco, Greene set out to visit the "very Catholic" city of Las Casas for Holy Week. The churches there had re-opened, but priests were not allowed to enter them or offer the sacraments. Chiapan Indians practised an animist form of Catholicism which led Greene to speculate, elsewhere, that Christians were apt to minimize the magic element in their own religion. Pre-Hispanic customs and superstitions lingered all through death-obsessed Mexico when Greene visited; they fascinated another English novelist, Malcolm Lowry, whose 1947 *Under the Volcano* unfolds in the shadow of Popocatepetl on the Mexican Day of the Dead. (The novel, with its alcoholic British diplomat, surely influenced Greene's *The Honorary Consul*). Ten years before Lowry, Greene had divined the Aztec skull beneath the skin, and in this extract he describes how the culture and superstitions of Mesoamerican Indians have survived in Catholicism.

"The Government are very uneasy about San Miguelito," the German bank manager said, scrambling over the rocks at the edge of Las Casas. The mountains of Chiapas stuck sharply up all round the city, perched there on its eight thousand foot plateau, parched and chilled alternately each day and night. Twenty-four churches rose like captive balloons above the one-story houses (but only seven were open and no priest was allowed inside), the mule tracks came down from the north and a single road ran south—to Tuxtla and the Government offices and the lounging pistoleros. It seemed odd that men like that should be troubled about a saint.

"San Miguelito?" I said.

He was astonished that I hadn't heard of San Miguelito. The news had spread as far as Tabasco a hundred miles away. He had owned a coffee finca himself on the borders of Tabasco and Chiapas, and the Indians had daily passed his gate, going to visit San Miguelito. Why, it was causing a religious revival: the government were so troubled they'd sent soldiers to seize the saint, but they hadn't captured him.

"What does he do?" I said.

"He recommends medicines—some of them Indian medicines and some the latest patent medicines from Mexico City."

"Is he a statue?"

"I don't know. I can't make it out—he's very small. Sometimes it sounds as if he's just a picture postcard. Of course they wouldn't let *me* see him."

The story was this: a poor Mexican farmer had for years kept San Miguelito (whatever he was) in a box. One day, about eighteen months ago, he had opened the box and San Miguelito had spoken to him in a high clear voice. He was so scared he ran all the way into the village of Bochil with the box, and there he had found four friends of his gathered together in a room. He had laid the box on the table and told them his story. Of course they didn't believe him: then one of them opened the box and the thin high voice came out of it. Soon after his astonishing discovery the farmer had died, and now San Miguelito was kept by his wife and his son in the small village of Sanoyo.

The German was a Protestant; he couldn't make head or tail of the thing; he really half believed the story—he knew one of the four men who was in that room when the farmer arrived with his box: he had listened to the pilgrims' tales. It couldn't be self-hypnotism—some of the patent medicines were ones no Indian could have heard of in the Chiapan wilds. There were no wires—apparently you could handle the box while San Miguelito talked. He had the reputation of speaking in German, French and English, as well as in Spanish and the Indian tongues. A lawyer from Las Casas had visited him and was convinced—but then the lawyer drank. What was one to believe, if one was an engineer, a bank manager and a Protestant?

Next morning I left at 6.30 by the only road. Sanoyo was only fifty kilometres away, but the car took nearly four hours. The road was appalling; it was more a mule track than a road, cut by crevices two feet deep, sprinkled with boulders. In the rains it is impassible; only aeroplanes can reach Las Casas then—and of course the mules from the north. Those tracks—as I bitterly knew—were so bad no rain could make them really worse. People who travelled that way by mule, the German said, came anyway—only necessity at the best of times dictated *that* journey. Yet going to Sanoyo by road was really worse. One dropped six thousand feet or more, circling the same mountain for forty minutes, bumping slowly round and round on the edge of the precipice, the same scenery on the opposite mountain recurring over and over again—as if one were a needle on a damaged record scraping the same track. A few bright blue birds mocked one like other people's happiness, and the scenery—the great pine forests dropping like curtains—was, I suppose, magnificent, but one was too sick and bruised to care.

It was Easter Sunday, but the only sign of the festival in the little drab village of Sanoyo was at the home of the saint. Some coloured paper streamers hung there, and when one had passed through the yard—a few chickens and pigs stirring the end-of-dry-season dust—one found in the small sala a decorated shrine to St. Anthony. The old mother slopped about in ancient gym shoes, tying up her white hair in a pink ribbon, and the chauffeur and I sat down on a bench and stared across at another bench where some villagers were patiently waiting. Out from an inner room—through the door I could see the end of a bed, a cheap woman's magazine and a paper streamer—came a little party of Indian women—tiny and bowed, old and hideous at twenty. With their cave-dwellers' faces and their long staffs they might have been Stone Age people emerging from forgotten caverns to pay their tribute to the Redeemer on Resurrection morning. One of them wept and wept, and a typewriter clattered with curious modernity in the bedroom. A marimba began to play in the yard among the chickens, and a rocket went off at each corner of the house in turn—it was impressive, a little asphyxiating, the tinkly pathetic music rising regularly to the explosion and sinking again; it was like the preparation for a great event, one's incredulity was assaulted. Suppose there was a miracle, suppose out of some box a voice did speak ... it was a horrifying thought that life could never be the same again; one couldn't go on living as one had been living. What happens afterwards to the people who are present at a genuine miracle?

But this wasn't a case like that. The music went on too long; I caught sight in the inner room of little conferences; the old woman slopped in and out weaving the pink ribbon in her hair. There was a young man in the bedroom who filled me with distrust—he had a humorous mouth; he looked more educated than the others; like a garage hand or a man in a radio shop. Radio ...?

Then after half an hour the son emerged. He wore a pink shirt which wasn't tucked in; his sleeves flapped clerically when he waved his hands; he had evasive eyes. He said the image wasn't there—it had gone to Villahermosa. We just sat on and took no notice. He asked whether I was a doctor—he hadn't liked doctors since the Medical Officer of Health in Tuxtla had come with soldiers to seize the saint. The saint had hidden in the woods and the disappointed soldiers had fired into the house—he showed the bullet marks on either side of the sala. I asked if we could see the saint: he flapped his pink sleeves and said he was in Villahermosa. We sat on. He brought out a visitors' book—there were twelve thousand names recorded: he brought out a pile of certificates of cures. There was always the same formula tapped out on his machine: "I Pedro Lopez certify that I was out of my mind (or had fits or worms in the head or something) and visited two doctors in my native place who said I was incurable. I came to Sanoyo and saw Señor—(I've forgotten the name). He gave me medicine and now I am quite cured." Then the signature and the witnesses' signatures and a passport photo of a brutal mestizo face— no mention of the saint.

The chauffeur got up and made a long speech. He said we knew the saint was in the bedroom; the señor lacked confidence in us, and yet how fully worthy we were of his trust. I wasn't a doctor, I was a foreigner who had come from England to see the saint. I was a Catholic and "muy religioso." It didn't seem to do much good—I caught a small child who came out of the bedroom and presented him with a rosary in a little glass box.

Another hour passed; the music had stopped and the fireworks; an old Indian came in to see the statue of St. Anthony and prayed and touched it with lemon leaves and went out. People from the village drifted in and stared at us and looked at the certificates and went out again into the fiery midday sun. A fat woman with a gross spotty face showed us a kind of primitive straight jacket and scars on her wrists— she had been cured of madness; the man in the pink shirt laid in my lap a bottle of maggots which had come out of a man's nose. The atmosphere was becoming unbearably clinical.

At last after two hours we wore them down. Resistance suddenly crumbled. The saint couldn't talk because it was Sunday, but we could see him. If we came back on Thursday, then the saint would talk ... We went into the bedroom and the son took casually down from a shelf—as if he were handling a grocery and not a miracle—one of those wooden Victorian tea caddies that are divided into two compartments. One compartment was empty; in the other had been glued the fretwork frame of a shrine, and a little picture of St. Michael was pasted at the back—the usual picture of the archangel slaying the dragon. Little balls of coloured silver paper filled the caddie, and among these a nail stuck up, and on the nail rested a little hollow head made, I think, of lead like a toy soldier. It certainly wasn't St. Michael's head—it was a woman's with crimped Grecian hair, an intaglio head. It was this which would give tongue—not on a Sunday, but next Thursday, though I think if I had been able to revisit the house, Thursday too would have proved an unpropitious day. This wasn't the setting for a miracle—there was something astute and amateurish about the whole thing ... We put an offering in the box—like the sick people who were not charged a centavo, and said goodbye.

On the way home we stopped for food at an Indian woman's cantina in Istapa and there we heard of a newer San Miguelito, who was also kept in a box, four leagues away by horse—he spoke even on a Sunday; the woman had heard him. So by this time I shouldn't be surprised if there were half a dozen San Miguelitos in Chiapas. The saint is cropping up like boils, and what else can you expect? The Mass is forbidden in the churches: only in the secrecy of a private house can the daily genuine miracle be performed, but religion will out, and when it is suppressed it breaks its way through in strange and sometimes poisonous forms.

July 2nd, 1938

A CATHOLIC ADVENTURER AND HIS MEXICAN JOURNAL

> Greene loathed Villahermosa; the town's stern-faced police
> had spread fear (the most important weapon in their armoury)
> among the inhabitants and subjected them to a brutal, anti-
> Catholic dogma. In such a place, Greene was delighted to
> encounter the local legend of Dr Fitzpatrick, a nineteenth-
> century Edinburgh-born adventurer. Greene may have found
> in Dr Fitzpatrick a trace of Robert Louis Stevenson, who was
> the novelist's cousin twice-removed. Like Greene, Stevenson
> was a literary buccaneer who travelled on the dangerous edge;
> the tense action across loch and moor, the thrilling flight
> through heather that Henry James had admired in *Kidnapped*
> would notably influence *The Power and the Glory*.

There are heroic adventures the world knows nothing of; diaries
recording incredible achievements rot in old drawers in the most
unlikely places. One can hardly imagine a more unlikely place than
Villahermosa, the capital of Tabasco, the little dirty tropical town set
down among the swamps and banana groves, cut off from the rest of
Mexico except by 'plane or boat—no railway and no roads, but it was
there I came on the manuscript diary of Dr. Fitzpatrick, a young Scots
Catholic who came to Mexico in 1863 seeking a practice to support
his wife Anna and his two-year-old baby Tom.

He had left the two of them in New Orleans, and his first attempt
to make a living petered miserably out in Tampico, now the great hot,
ugly oil port. Then came his first stupendous adventure of which the
record, alas, has been lost! There remains in the existing diary only
the brief statement: "A year ago today I left Tampico with forty-seven
cents, to walk to New Orleans"—three hundred odd miles to the
Mexican border, and more than twice that distance more through
Texas and Louisiana. He stayed in New Orleans a few months only:
stubborn and Scotch, he set out again, this time to the Republic of

Panama where, for some unknown reason, he imagined there were good prospects for a doctor. From this time on we have the day-to-day entries of his disillusionment and laconic despair.

As a Scottish Catholic he was shocked by the condition of the Church in Panama: as a lonely young man of thirty-one, who had very little Spanish, he found himself consorting more and more with the disreputable and kindly Padre Rey. His brief entries build up a pathetic picture of his disapproval and his grudging friendship for this bizarre priest who lived with his wife and daughter (he said in excuse that he had married her before he became a priest) and kept live mice in a glass lamp. Stories about the Bishop of Panama reached Dr. Fitzpatrick's ears ... It wasn't the sort of Catholicism he was used to in Scotland.

And all the time his money was draining away and no patients came. On Christmas Day he was reduced to eight dollars, and he felt an intolerable loneliness, thinking of "my beloved Anna and dear little Tom." He posted letters which she would probably never receive, and got none himself. Then at last, with the help of Padre Rey, he found a patient, and earned enough money to take his passage on a boat for Salvador—it was at least a little nearer to the States.

Then began the second great adventure. Salvador was at war with Guatemala, but in spite of that, without money and without arms and without Spanish, he took a horse and rode 997 miles (he is always exact in his calculations) to the Atlantic, seeking in vain for a home and a practice—across Salvador (arrested as a spy and released), across Guatemala (meeting the Indian dictator with his soldiers in the field) and into Mexico, right across Chiapas, climbing the eight thousand feet to cold Las Casas, then down again into Tabasco and the appalling tropical heat, and so to the sea. There is nothing in the diary to show he was conscious of the magnitude of his adventure—Indian superstitions, native medicines described with medical frankness, so many miles covered—most of the entries are Scotch in their brevity and matter-of-factness. Only at moments when he thinks of Anna and Tom (he doesn't even know if they are still alive: he left them in the midst of the American Civil War) does the individuality of the young homesick man break through into the diary. Once he sang "God Save the Queen" to keep his spirits up, climbing a mountain in Chiapas.

It is pleasant to know that he found his way safely back to New Orleans, that his wife and baby were well, and that eventually they all found prosperity—in Villahermosa of all places. His reputation as a doctor extended to Mexico City and across the Gulf to Merida: he was called in by Porfirio Diaz[1] to treat his wife, and died in 1905, in Campeche—a town he had always hated—on his way to see the Governor of Yucatan. There are photographs in the Mexican sala where the unpublished record lies on a shelf—Anna, a middle-aged woman in a crinoline, with one of those calm Victorian faces that hide years of the wildest anxieties; "dear little Tom", looking like a Dean with a fierce black spade beard; and Dr. Fitzpatrick himself, old and stern, with a beard as fierce as Tom's, wearing a long frock-coat. The young Scotsman who had tramped from Tampico with forty-seven cents, who had ridden those thousand miles to the Atlantic, sleeping in Indian huts and depending for his life on the charity of a plate of beans and a cup of native coffee, turned into this rather awe-inspiring figure, a man who never wore a shirt more than twice and who rode about the streets of the tropical town, among the buzzards and the mosquitoes, in the long dark broadcloth he would have worn in Edinburgh.

August 13th, 1938

THE DARK VIRGIN

"It is doubtful", Evelyn Waugh commented of high-altitude Mexico City, "how much humankind can become properly at ease in this climate." The Mexican capital (rudely renamed Make Sicko City) is now the greatest urban concentration in history; its 950 square miles cover an area roughly three times the size of New York City and its inhabitants suffer grievous air and water pollution. (*No hay remedio*, they say: "There's nothing to be done.") Yet thousands of impoverished Mexicans continue to stream into the capital each day in search of work. In their battered straw stetsons and with reddened faces, these rural dispossessed are derisively referred to as *los indios*. They worship the dark-skinned Virgin of Guadalupe, Mexico's first indigenous saint, and are descendants of Aztec and other Mexica peoples. In Greene's day, Mexico was still largely an indigenous Indian civilization, and the novelist typically identifies with the Virgin of Guadalupe as the protector of the Indian poor. During the presidency of Lázaro Cárdenas (a protégé of President Calles), Garrido Canabal and his Red Shirts had tried, but failed, to destroy the Guadalupe shrine.

Guadalupe—a quarter of an hour's tram ride from the Cathedral, in a suburb which retains the form of a village, as some parts of London do—is not merely the most important shrine in Mexico City: it is the centre of the nation's devotion. The plain formal eighteenth century church stands in a little plaza where a market is held every day of the week—ices and fruit and flowers, little sweet corncakes cooked while you watch and wrapped in coloured papers like crackers, blue Guadalupe glass the colour of poison bottles, small crude toys. Outside the Chapel of the Well, a spring which is said to have flowed from under the feet of the Virgin, are stacks of empty whisky bottles. In the church the miraculous serape hangs above the altar—the dark-skinned Virgin bending her head with a grace and kindliness you will find nowhere in mortal Mexico.

She appeared first at Amecameca, fifty miles away, but no one paid her any attention: then on December 9th, 1531, an Indian peasant, Juan Diego, was climbing Tepeyac Hill, at the foot of which the shrine now stands. The Virgin appeared to him among the rocks—there was music, suddenly, and light—she called him "my son" and told him to carry a message to Bishop Zumarraga that he was to build a shrine where she might watch and guard the Indians. (Zumarraga was the Bishop who, to the permanent grief of archæologists, burnt the Aztec manuscripts in the market place of Tlaltelolco, the town to which Diego was going to receive instruction.)

It is as well to remember how revolutionary this vision must have seemed. It was only ten years since Mexico City had fallen finally to Cortes, the country was not yet subdued, and one wonders what kind of greeting the average Spanish adventurer would have given an Indian who claimed to have been addressed as "my son" by the Mother of God. The legend, Mexican politicians say, was invented by the Church to enslave the Indian mind, but if indeed it had been invented at that period, the purpose would have been very different. The Virgin claimed a church from which she might guard her Indians—from the Spanish conquerors. The legend gave the Indian self-respect: it gave him a hold over his conqueror: it was a liberating legend.

The Bishop, of course, disbelieved Diego. Bishops share the prejudices of their race and time. "My son" may have stuck in the Bishop's throat, just as the encyclical *De Rerum Novarum* later stuck in the gullet of the Bishop of San Luis Potosi, so that he kept the copies stacked in his cellar for fear of Communism, where a priest found them after Carranza's rising[2]. On Sunday, December 10th (the legend is well dated) the Virgin appeared again to Diego on Tepeyac Hill and he asked her to send some more important messenger—some Spaniard, he may have implored her—whom the Bishop would believe. She might have appeared to Cortes himself who could have commanded anything.

But one wonders what would have been the future of that vision if it had been sent to the Conqueror instead of to the Conquered. A rich shrine would have been built, but would the Indians have attended it? Eventually it would have been closed like every church in Mexico. But this shrine of Guadalupe, even at the height of the persecution, remained open—no Government dared to rob the Indian of his Virgin, and it broke the career of the only man who ever threatened it. A few years ago, when Garrido Canabal, the dictator of Tabasco, arrived in the capital accompanied by his Red Shirts to take his seat as Minister of Agriculture in Cardenas's cabinet, he gave secret orders to his men that the shrine was to be destroyed, as the Tabascan churches had already been. A bomb was flung and failed to damage the image, and Garrido was driven from Mexico to exile in Costa Rica.

So the Virgin sent the Indian peasant back to Bishop Zumarraga, and the bishop cautiously demanded a sign. For the third time Diego listened to the Virgin who told him to return next day, but next day Diego's uncle was very ill and he forgot—or more likely the *fact* of the dying man seemed more true than a vision he may himself have discounted when the bishop talked, full of the slowness and wisdom and sane scepticism of the church authority. On Tuesday, the 12th, he had to return to Tlaltelolco to fetch a priest to his uncle, but he was afraid of that particular stony path he associated with his vision, and took a different way. As if he could escape on one path more than another. He showed the same materialism as the sceptical Catholics today who discount the vision because *this* Virgin was dark-skinned—

as if the Mother of God, released like her Son from the flesh, belongs to one continent or race more than another.

Diego could not escape. The Virgin blocked his new path too, without reproach. No vision of the Mother of God has ever been associated with the idea of punishment. She told him his uncle was already well and directed him to go to the top of the hill to gather roses from the rocks and take them to the Bishop. He wrapped the roses in his serape and when he opened it before the Bishop, the image of the Virgin was there, stamped on the cloth, just as it hangs above the altar today.

An old Spanish lady, Señora B., was showing me Guadalupe, sceptically. She took me through the vestry into the small room where the votive paintings are hung: thanks to the Virgin, expressed in little vivid primitive daubs, like the paintings of talented children, explained in short ungrammatical sentences: a wife in bed watching her drunken husband: little men with awkward hands and pistols shooting at each other. Afterwards we climbed the steep winding steps which now go up Tepeyac Hill to the shrine built on the spot of the Vision. At every corner photographers stood with old hooded cameras and antique screens—an early steamship, balloons, improbable aeroplanes out of Jules Verne, and the swans and lakes and roses and *châteaux* of a nostalgic period. Little braziers burned, and there was a smell of corncake all the way up. Near the chapel is the rich man's cemetery, huge tombs with Spanish coats of arms in lichened stone, huddling for safety near the peasants' shrine. There is no earth on Tepeyac Hill: it has to be carried up by human labour: and every grave must be carved out of solid rock.

The old lady sought for her ancestors among lanes of mausoleums like those of a new building estate where every house is different. She had lost all her money, lived in a small bed-sitting-room where she entertained her grandchildren every Wednesday, the kettle boiling beside the bed: she had immense courage and vivacity and the will to endure. She was the descendant of a general who had fought for Itúrbide[3] and independence from Spain, and then had been exiled by Iturbide when he took the crown. But General B. could not be kept out of his country, he secretly returned and moving from place to place, he stamped his features on the children of Mexico. At his death, according to his wishes, his heart went to Guadalajara where he met his wife, and his right arm to Lerma where he won his victory, and the rest of his body to Guadalupe. And Señora B. retained the panache and the pride, but the aristocratic attitude, baulked of authority, had become bitter, defiant, useless. The enemy of Cardenas, she was also the enemy of his opponent Cedillo[4], whose father had been an Indian peasant on *her* family's estates in San Luis Potosi. She was too proud to choose between two evils—she was typical of many Spaniards of birth who have simply withdrawn, into bed-sitting-rooms and small hotels.

She was a Catholic, too, but with aristocratic scepticism. She wouldn't believe in Diego's vision and the miraculous image—it was a popular fantasy. She withdrew, as in politics, from the source of life. She for one, I am sure, would have been more ready to accept the vision if it had come to the conqueror and not to the peasant. Nevertheless she knelt, saying her Hail Mary; she didn't believe—but among Catholics even the sceptical are courteous.

December 31st, 1938

OUR LADY AND HER ASSUMPTION

"The Only Figure of Perfect Human Love"

At the war's end it seemed that Europe had entered an "unmiraculous age" when the time of Catholic saints and miracles was over and a dour new religiosity had emerged: atomic science. Nevertheless, reinvigorated cults linked with the Virgin Mary and the Saints gave the lie to claims that materialist science was carrying all before it. The visitation of the Madonna to an Italian bus inspector and his three children outside Rome on 12th April 1947 especially fascinated Greene. And in this essay he looks at the occurrence of religious mysteries—sorrowing Virgins, weeping Madonnas—that defy comprehension. Greene knew very well that our capacity for credulity is infinite; in more recent times the spiritualist medium Doris Stokes was able to fill to capacity the London Palladium with her demonstrations of clairaudience or the ability to hear the dead—proof of the enduring popularity of what G. K. Chesterton called "mediums and moonshine". Nevertheless there are many who claim that God reveals himself by suspending the laws of science, and Greene I think was among them.

There is one saint in the calendar of the Church who has never been associated with the idea of punishment: even justice is alien to her, compared with the ideas of mercy and love. She is the one whom Catholics know as Our Lady.

Yet it is around this figure that the bitterest conflict has always been waged. No statues in Puritan England were more certain to be destroyed than hers, and the same was true in Spain in the 1930s. Ministers in their pulpits may question the divinity of Christ and cause no stir outside a few country rectories—but when the doctrine of the Assumption, which has been established as a feast of the

Church for more than a thousand years, is defined as a dogma, the Archbishops of Canterbury and York claim that the division of Christendom has been widened[5]. They believe in the resurrection of the dead—but to suggest that an actual resurrection has already taken place seems to them blasphemous. No storm was raised when, a hundred years ago, Newman wrote: "Original sin had not been found in her, by the wear of her senses, and the waste of her frame and the decrepitude of years, propagating death. She died, but her death was a mere fact, not an effect; and, when it was over, it ceased to be." Temporally there were other issues: the Protestant churches were worried by the idea of evolution, even the age of the earth was a cause of scandal because it was believed to contradict Genesis. But the conflict of science and religion always passes sooner or later: what remains is this mysterious savage war around the only figure of perfect human love.

What is the explanation? One theologian has explained it, for our generation, as a distrust of the concrete. We are so used to abstractions. Words like Democracy and Liberty can be used in quite opposite senses without arousing attention: they go in and out of our ears like air. So with religious belief. The Supreme Being, the Trinity, the Creator of all things, such phrases may once have excited thought, but they do so no longer. Even the concrete name Christ has become so diluted, into the Great Teacher, the First Communist, and the like, that only a small amount of opposition is raised by the idea that Christ is God—it is rather like saying Truth is God. But the statement that Mary is the Mother of God remains something shocking, paradoxical, physical.

But it is from that statement that all Christianity springs. To quote Newman again, "When once we have mastered the idea that Mary bore, suckled, and handled the Eternal in the form of a child, what limit is conceivable to the rush and flood of thoughts which such a doctrine involves?" The flood of thoughts may sometimes have taken bizarre channels, but the Church is slow and careful: tales are allowed plenty of time to wither of themselves, and there is surely small sign of impetuosity in the proclamation in 1854 of the Immaculate Conception which was already part of the accepted teaching of the Church, in the East and the West and in Africa, within a few years of the death of St. John. As for the Assumption, which even unguided human logic might detect as an essential effect of the Immaculate Conception, the Church has waited longer still.

Our opponents sometimes claim that no belief should be held dogmatically which is not explicitly stated in scripture (ignoring that it is only on the authority of the Church we recognize certain Gospels and not others as true). But the Protestant churches have themselves accepted such dogmas as the Trinity for which there is no such precise authority in the Gospels. St. John wrote, "There is much else besides that Jesus did; if all of it were put in writing I do not think the world itself would contain the books which would have to be written"; and it is our claim that Tradition alone—founded on the Apostles' teaching, analyzed and reflected on through the ages by the Church, under the guidance of the Holy Spirit promised by Christ— illumines the full and true meaning of the Scriptures.

From the Scriptures themselves we know very little of Our Lady beyond the first appalling facts of the Annunciation and the Virgin Birth. St. Luke's Gospel is sometimes known as Our Lady's, for St. Luke gives details of the Visitation and the Birth that could only have come from Mary's account of them. St. Matthew's Gospel complements his account with the Flight into Egypt. St. John, with whom, so tradition declares, she spent the remainder of her life after the Crucifixion, tells us how Christ performed for her his first miracle at the wedding feast of Cana, how she stood at the foot of the Cross and how Christ entrusted her to the disciple whom he loved. From the Acts we learn that she was present with the Apostles in the upper room at Pentecost, and afterwards there is complete silence—a few legends, that is all. "Her departure made no noise in the world," Newman wrote. "The Church went about her common duties, preaching, converting, suffering; there were persecutions, there was fleeing from place to place, there were martyrs, there were triumphs; at length the rumour spread abroad that the Mother of God was no longer upon earth. Pilgrims went to and fro; they sought for her relics, but they found them not; did she die at Ephesus? Or did she die at Jerusalem? Reports varied; but her tomb could not be pointed out, or if it was found it was open."

Legend tells how the Apostles were suddenly gathered together round her deathbed, how they buried her and on the third day found her tomb empty, but the dogma of the Assumption does not demand that we should believe these details of her end. We are only asked to believe what the Church in historical memory has always believed, that, just as in her case the taint of original sin was never allowed to touch her ("our tainted nature's solitary boast," Wordsworth wrote), so the corruption of the body, which we believe is the effect of original sin, never occurred: she is soul and glorified body (whatever that may be) in heaven (wherever that can be found).

Scripture, tradition, legend—all these contribute either to our knowledge of Mary, or to our knowledge of how men regarded her. In her case, unlike that of any other saint there is another source; she alone has consistently, throughout history up to the present day, appeared to men. There has been an undrying flow of visions: she is a woman of a hundred geographical titles—Lourdes, La Salette, Carmel, Fatima, Guadalupe, Lima. The Church has never demanded that we should believe in any of these visions as an article of faith. Some of the visions, just as some of the legends, the Church has even condemned. Those regarded as worthy of credence are not confined

to one continent or one race. Some go back beyond the period of
proper investigation, like that of Our Lady of Walsingham in England
whose shrine was visited barefoot one snowbound winter by Henry
VIII and was afterwards destroyed by the same king's henchmen.
The legend tells us that Our Lady appeared to a noble widow and
commanded her to build a shrine after the style of her own house in
Nazareth. The work went awry. During one night therefore Our Lady
built the house herself with the help of angels. Of course we need
give no credence to the legend as it has come down to us, but the
persistence and purity of the devotion around this shrine—a devotion
that touched even the sceptical Erasmus—which continues today in
the pilgrimages to the restored shrine, suggests at least the possibility
of some genuine vision behind the myth. Can one write so beautifully
about a lie as the anonymous sixteenth century author of the *Lament
over Walsingham*?

> *Bitter bitter Oh to behold*
> *the grass to grow*
> *Where the walls of Walsingham*
> *so stately did show;*
> *Such were the works of Walsingham*
> *while she did stand;*
> *Such are the wrecks as now do show*
> *of that holy land.*
> *Level level with the ground*
> *the towers do lie*
> *Which with their golden glittering tops*
> *pierced once to the sky ...*
> *Weep weep O Walsingham*
> *whose days are nights,*
> *Blessings turned to blasphemies,*
> *holy deeds to dispites.*
> *Sin is where Our Lady sat*
> *Heaven turnéd to Hell,*

Satan sits where Our Lord did sway,
Walsingham O farewell.

If the origin of Walsingham goes back into those deep medieval shadows that contrast with the clarity and lucidity of the primitive age, the vision of the Virgin of Guadalupe is established almost as exactly as the nineteenth century visions of Lourdes and La Salette, or the twentieth century vision of Fatima. [...] The Virgin of Guadalupe has the features of an Indian. We know nothing of a resurrected body save that it has substance (St. Thomas put his hand in Our Lord's wounds) and yet can pass through the wall of a room, that Christ after his resurrection was sometimes recognized immediately by his disciples and yet sometimes could walk beside them unknown. The Virgin appeared to Bernadette as a girl little older than herself, to the children of Fatima as a woman, to an Indian as an Indian.

In spite of the miracles of Lourdes, attested by a sceptic like Zola and a scientist like Alexis Carrel, we are apt to think of this as an unmiraculous age. The miracles of Lourdes are cures—we can persuade ourselves that science will one day explain them (Carrel, who witnessed the instantaneous cure of a girl dying of tubercular peritonitis, tried unsuccessfully to persuade himself that his diagnosis had been at fault). But this is an age of visions as well as cures: if we are entering a new Dark Age we are being given the same consolations as our ancestors. Since the defeat of the Turks at Lepanto the battle for Christianity has never been more critical, and sometimes it seems as though the supernatural were gathering its forces for our support, and whom should we expect in the vanguard but Our Lady? For the attack on the Son has always come through the Mother. She is the keystone of Christian doctrine. If you wish to discredit the divinity of Christ you discredit the Virgin Birth; if you wish to discredit the manhood of Christ, you discredit the motherhood of Our Lady.

One vision which is likely to be regarded as credible by the Church (let me emphasize again that no Catholic is bound to believe even in the vision of St. Bernadette, for a Saint can be deceived) is that of the Tre Fontane, a cave on a hillside near Rome opposite a Trappist monastery that is said to be the scene of St. Paul's execution. Now a rough path made by pilgrims runs along the slope of the hill among the low eucalyptus trees to a small clearing and a cave sparkling with votive offerings. Cripples sell candles along the way, and when I was last there dozens of children from a war orphanage, each child without a leg or an arm, were helping each other across the clearing to where women knelt and scooped into their handkerchiefs the earth they believed had been pressed by Mary's feet. On April 12th, 1947, a Roman bus inspector, Bruno Cornacchiola, a Communist and renegade Catholic, was walking in these woods with his three children: he was preparing a speech attacking the title of the Mother of God. His children called to him to help them find their ball. "I went over," he said. "What do I see? Gianfranco on his knees at the entrance to the grotto, his hands joined. He murmurs, 'Beautiful lady, beautiful lady.' I call Isola. 'Come here. What is your brother saying? What is there in there?' 'It's nothing,' says the child and at the same moment there she is on the ground in the same attitude, saying the same words as Gianfranco. I understand nothing. 'Carlo, tell me what is this and what are you playing at?' 'I don't know,' replies the child, and there he is on his knees too. 'Beautiful lady, beautiful lady,' he says. I am astounded, and it is as though two hands are passed over my eyes; a veil has fallen. A great light illuminates the grotto, and in the middle there appears …"

I quote no more because, as so often in such cases, the human description of the vision becomes unreal, stilted, academic. (We judge its authenticity partly by its effect on the family concerned.) If St.

John of the Cross fails to convey his vision, how can a child or a bus conductor convey theirs? They are forced back on trite words, pious phrases, "I am She who lies in the bosom of the Divine Trinity," and the like. To me almost the only convincing words any of these visions have spoken were those reported by the child Bernadette. There had been many sermons and much talk on the new dogma of the Immaculate Conception and she had no idea of its meaning, until that girl of about her own age appeared to her in the Pyrennean cave and explained, "*I* am the Immaculate Conception," as much as to say, "This doctrine of the Second Eve which theologians have been discussing for 1,600 years is as simple as that—it is me, whom you know, that's all." We can look for no enlargements of knowledge from these visions. But there is a common feature in all her appearances, the appeal for prayer and yet more prayer. Her message is as simple as that, and it may seem unimportant unless we have some realization of the terrible force of prayer, the mysterious untapped power able to move mountains.

What a strange distance, like a stellar space, cold and incomprehensible, separates the child Bernadette or the boy Francesco at Fatima from indignant theologians who deplore the dogma of the Assumption as "an added difficulty to reunion" of all Christian churches. It may be "a difficulty", but those children have *seen* the glorified body, and you will not persuade them to suppress their vision because it is tactless, because it may offend a few dignitaries of an alien faith. If the dogma had not been proclaimed now it would still one day have been proclaimed. The Church has waited nearly twelve hundred years since the feast of the Assumption was appointed by the Synod of Salzburg in 800, and the Synod had waited more than six hundred years since the first written reference to the common belief. We might have waited another thousand years, but the Church has decided otherwise.

It is legitimate, of course, to speculate why this precise moment in history has been chosen. I can write only as an uninstructed Catholic. Because the doctrines of Christ's nature as God and Man are walled about by the doctrine of the Annunciation and the Virgin Birth, so that it is not too much to say that the whole of Christianity to this day lies in Our Lady's womb, it is to her that recourse has always been had in times of crisis. So it was through all the terrible storms of the sixteenth century when the Turks seemed on the point of conquering Europe: appropriately Pius V instituted the feast day of the Most Holy Rosary in thanksgiving for the great victory of Lepanto. And now, when a yet heavier threat lies upon our borders, perhaps the proclamation of the new dogma will help the devotion of millions. Devotion means simply an expression of love, and if we love enough, even in human terms, we gain courage.

This would be no argument, of course, for proclaiming a novel belief, but a dogma is only a definition of an old belief. It restricts the area of truth at the expense of legend or heresy, and the greatest definitions of the Church, accepted alike by Protestants and Catholics—the nature of Christ, the doctrine of the Trinity—were definitions drawn up to exclude heresies within the Church itself.

In our day there are no obvious signs of heretical beliefs within the Church concerning the Assumption of Our Lady and therefore it was believed by some Catholics that to proclaim the dogma was unnecessary. But Catholics today cannot remain quite untouched by the general heresy of our time, the unimportance of the individual. Today the human body is regarded as expendable material, something to be eliminated wholesale by the atom bomb, a kind of anonymous carrion. After the First World War crosses marked the places where the dead lay, Allied and enemy: lights burned continually in the capitals of Europe over the graves of the unknown warriors. But no crosses today mark the common graves into which the dead of London and Berlin were shovelled, and Hiroshima's memorial is the outline of a body photographed by the heat flash on asphalt. The definition of the Assumption proclaims again the doctrine of our Resurrection, the eternal destiny of each human body, and again it is the history of Mary which maintains the doctrine in its clarity. The Resurrection of Christ can be regarded as the Resurrection of a God, but the Resurrection of Mary foreshadows the Resurrection of each one of us.

February 3rd, 1951

Graham Greene on patrol with French troops at Phat Diem, a coastal port near Hanoi, Vietnam, 1951.

CATHOLICS AT WAR

Extracts from an Indo-China Journal (1954)

At this time—1954—Greene felt that Vietnamese Catholics presented an equally valid opposition to the French as did the Communist Viet Minh under Ho Chi Minh (whom Greene interviewed), or indeed the nationalists commanded by emperor Bao Dai. Bui Chu (which Greene visited) is one of the two bishoprics in the north of Indo-China, the other being Phat Diem. The French, among them the Colonel Sizaire mentioned here (commander of the Franco-Vietnamese forces in the south), were now in the process of leaving Vietnam for good. It is ironic, given Greene's attack on America's role in Indo-China, and later Vietnam, contained in *The Quiet American*, that the novelist first went to Indo-China as a reporter for the New York-based *Life*. The American magazine had featured Greene on its cover when *The End of the Affair* was published in 1951, and the novelist had written articles for them subsequently, including "Our Lady and Her Assumption".

January 8th

At 9.50 I took a plane from Hanoi to Nam Dinh. Here, two years ago, I had stayed with Colonel Sezaire. From here I had slipped into burning, besieged Phat Diem in a French landing craft carrying Vandenburg and his black-clothed Commando of ex-Viet Minh prisoners—Vandenburg, with his animal face and dangling hangman's hands (a few weeks later he was murdered by his own Commando before they deserted). Nothing in the delta ever seems to change—not even the gunfire.

I was on my way to Bui Chu, the Annamite bishopric on the edge of Phat Diem—the first region to be handed over by the French to the Viet Nam forces, a premature decision, for two battalions deserted to the enemy with their new American weapons, and the French had temporarily to return to clean up the mess.

Some hours had to be passed before my plane to Bui Chu and these I spent with a French colonel, who took me to a performance of *Le Cid*, in French, given by the equivalent of E.N.S.A.[6] to the students and teachers of the Nam Dinh schools. It was not such an odd choice as might appear, for the Vietnamese theatre, too, is heroic and the costumes were less alien to the Vietnamese idea of theatre than contemporary ones would have been. All the same, there was a continuous ripple of laughter—perhaps some of it was caused by the dialogue, which it is difficult for even an Englishman to appreciate (*honneur* and *gloire* sounding regularly like the tolling of a bell), but probably more was caused by the presence of real women on the stage (as unknown in the Eastern theatre as it was in Elizabethan England) and by the abrupt and exaggerated changes of gesture and tone. When a man actually knelt at a woman's feet the laughter rose higher than ever.

At 3.50 I caught my plane on to Bui Chu—ten minutes by plane but six hours by road if the road had been open, because of the loops of the Red River. The Bishop of Bui Chu was a very different character from the neighbouring Bishop of Phat Diem, younger, with a greater knowledge of the world outside than the former Trappist monk. The Bishop of Phat Diem was only interested in building more and more churches (for which he hadn't the priests): the conditions of the market, the lack of a hospital—this meant little to him, and he was interested in education only in so far as it produced priests. I did not find him a vain man, but his position was that of a medieval Bishop—the temporal ruler of his diocese. When he drove in his jeep down the long narrow street of Phat Diem, his fingers raised in benediction, impassive as a statue, he reminded me of an ancient mural, in which only the significant lines have escaped the destruction of time, the raised fingers, the tassel on the episcopal hat. The Bishop of Bui Chu belonged to our day and world—and our day and world includes the pockmark of bullets on the seminary wall which the Viet Minh attacked in June. They broke in at night and carried away four priests (two of them Belgian, whom I remembered meeting in 1952 and with whom I discussed English literature). They fired, too, into the sisters' chapel and killed four sisters—one falling dead under the statue of Our Lady (the wall still bore the mark of the bullets).

The guns rumbled across the fields of rice in the soft gold evening light. An old priest said to me, "After that I began to learn French."

There is a terrible squalor about war in these days: men emerging from holes, bearded, dirty, wearing the chevrons of their rank wherever is most convenient; the little forgotten hospitals like those of Bui Chu, served by a few priests and sisters, without enough bandages; the wounded women; the men with their feet gashed on the bamboo points of the Viet Minh defences. Four wounded had come in today and two had died. It was part of the day's work, but there was no clean room for doctor and nurse to retire to, no bath, no easy chair, no change from the smell of wounds.

One of the priests, a young man with a squint, pale gums and several gold teeth, took me to his room and gave me tiny glasses of sweet altar wine. He had been learning English from one of the Belgian fathers who was kidnapped and he was anxious to practise. He was suffering, he said, from "*faiblesse générale*," and could do little work. He was my constant companion for two days, giggling and trying to copy my English pronunciation, carrying on his lessons up to the last possible moment, in the jeep on the landing ground.

January 9ᵗʰ

Mass in the cathedral at 6.45, after being woken by gunfire before daybreak. It was strange and moving, in the big cathedral, to be the only European. The grace of the Annamite priest and his vestments, everything the same and yet all the faces so different. The Church seemed to give a model for the politicians—Christianity can survive without Europe. Why not trust the people?

After Mass I was pulled away before I could get my breakfast by two priests who wished to be given a small lesson in English.

During the morning visited the refugee camp—six hundred people who had been evacuated from the villages captured in June by the Viet Minh. In one hut were five families separated by hangings. In one tiny compartment hung a picture of Our Lady, with a bleeding heart, and Bao Dai.

The commandant in charge of the troops in the Bui Chu area. A Vietnamese with a tough, sympathetic face, full of confidence, a Buddhist. Under his leadership, to all intents Bui Chu was independent. Only one French artillery post remained, otherwise not only the troops but the Church was Vietnamian. Could they fight? To answer that question they brought me to the fortified village of Thui-nai.

One approached it by a jeep along the narrow causeways between the canals. The Commandant thought of sending ahead of us a mine-detecting patrol, and a few minutes before we arrived they found a mine, enclosed in a wooden box with a piece of wood over the detonator to try to make it undetectable. A mine of Chinese manufacture with the instructions printed in Chinese. Why is it one is not more thankful for life? The commander of the patrol went, later, to the Bishop's residence to receive his thanks for saving the life of his guest, but it is too difficult to thank God with any sincerity for this gift of life.

The fortified village of Thui-nai was the most impressive thing I have seen in the Indo-China war. Here was a popular Dien Bien Phu made with the spades and pickaxes of local men: a maze of mud walls and firing emplacements that extended right into the church itself, mud ramps standing in the aisle for the last stand. Since August the village, with no aid from proper troops, had beaten off nine night attacks by the Viet Minh, the last on December 30th. Everyone who could walk was in the militia. The church was gay with yellow Vietnam flags, and in the Square, for my inspection, in orderly ranks, stood the whole village: small girls of twelve carried knives and wore hand grenades in their belts. One home-made mortar, a Bren gun, a few Stens—for the rest they had to fight with old rifles and knives and grenades—there were plenty of these. The Commandant was young, smart, imaginative. He had organized his own information office: the village Roll of Honour, charts of organization, photographs. As we sat with him at tea, the squinting priest said to me, "He is a commandant without rank or pay, who eats his mother's rice in return for fighting his father's enemies." If all villages were as homogeneous as this and as well organized, there would be no problem in the delta, but here was the enormous advantage that every soul in the village was Catholic. They felt a personal threat.

I think that the loss of the two battalions had been good for Bui Chu. It brought the threat home and killed complacency. Catholicism had not been enough. Now they were being encouraged again. The commandant of the 46th Viet Minh Regiment had come in the day before to surrender, carrying with him plans for the capture of Bui Chu. He was surprised to find himself received by a Vietnam commandant and a Vietnam captain (a young intelligence officer with a kind of fanatical smartness, who had once been a Franciscan). The major was following one of his own captains who had surrendered three weeks before. Both men were Communists—not nationalists caught up in the Viet Minh camp and disillusioned. Something was badly wrong with the 46th Regiment, and nobody knew what. Had these men offended the political commissars attached to each battalion? We are too apt to forget the strain in the enemy's camp, seeing only our own tensions and doubts.

After lunch, I flew round the Bui Chu defences in a Morain plane piloted by a young medical student called up from Hanoi University. Only one post of artillery flew a French flat with the Vietnamese—a bird's-eye view of independence. When I returned, the Bishop put his head into my room and asked whether I would like "a small promenade." The promenade turned out to be the consecration of a new church in a village which had become entirely Catholic a year ago. As the Bishop moved around the wall scattering holy water, while the guns grumbled like an aching tooth, one was aware that the political or material motive here for becoming Catholic was very small.

After that, tea with the *Chef de Province*, and the awful tiredness that comes from hospitality—the strain of politeness and friendliness in the absence of companionship. Then one longs most to be with the people one loves, the people with whom it is possible to be silent.

January 10th

The conversions certainly go on. Before Mass this morning, in the Bishop's chapel, there were fifteen baptisms, thirteen of them in one family. It was the patronal feast, and a Mass more gay than any I have seen outside Vienna. The Bishop was robed to the music of violins, gay tinkly music like an eighteenth-century gavotte. The altar boys carried the vestments with a ballet grace: even the candles on the altar seemed to dance. One was worlds away from the dull bourgeois

Masses of France and England, the best clothes and the beadle, and the joyless faces and the Gregorian chants. This was a Mass to be enjoyed, and why not? The sacrament is too serious for us to compete in seriousness. Under the enormous shadow of the cross it is better to be gay.

Later, the school children performed a long heroic play in verse as incomprehensible to me as *The Cid* had been to the Vietnamese, and then there was a banquet to all the priests and schoolmasters and officers. I had to leave in the middle of it to catch my plane back to Hanoi, and the squinting priest went with me, learning English to the last.

NOTES

1. Porfirio Diaz, Mexican president 1876-80 and 1884-1911.
2. Venustiano Carranza, Mexican president 1917-1920.
3. Agustín de Itúrbide, Mexican general who made himself Emperor as Agustín I (1822-3).
4. General Saturnino Cedillo, the strongman of San Luis Potosi, was interviewed by Greene in 1938: "an Indian general in an obscure state of a backward country."
5. In 1950, Pius XIII defined the dogma of Mary's bodily assumption.
6. Entertainment National Service Association (jocularly known during the Second World War as 'Every Night Something Awful').

two

FICTION

23/30 December 1978

Christmas Reading

HOW FATHER QUIXOTE BECAME A MONSIGNOR

"The piece I am sending you"—Greene wrote to Tom Burns on 13 November 1978—"is the first chapter of a novel which probably will never be completed. Perhaps you should describe it as the first chapter of a novel in progress. I think that might arouse more interest than calling it a short story." Burns was delighted to publish the story, but Greene was upset by his eventual choice of illustrations, which showed a fat, pear-shaped priest wearing a foolish grin. "Father Quixote was not a silly little plump figure and anyone who had read the piece with any understanding would have known he was if anything meagre", Greene wrote to Burns, adding: "I don't like illustration of fiction unless it's done by a competent hand like the illustrator of Sherlock Holmes. Perhaps *The Tablet* needs a little more taste in its productions."

It happened this way. Father Quixote had ordered his solitary lunch from his housekeeper and set off to buy wine at a local cooperative eight kilometres away from El Toboso on the main road to Valencia.

Graham Greene enjoying a glass of wine with Father Durán, the model for
Father Quixote, at home in Antibes, early 1980s.

It was a day when the heat stood and quivered on the dry fields, and there was no air-conditioning in his little six-year-old Fiat Five. As he drove he thought sadly of the day when he would have to find a new car. A dog's years can be multiplied by seven to equal a man's, and by that calculation his car would still be in early middle age, but he noticed how already his parishioners began to regard his Fiat as almost senile. "You can't trust it, Don Quixote," they would warn him and he could only reply, "It has been with me through many bad days, and I pray God that it may survive me." So many of his prayers had remained unanswered that he had hopes that this one prayer of his had lodged all the time like wax in the Eternal ear.

He could see where the main road lay by reason of the small dust puffs raised by the passing cars. As he drove he worried about the fate of what he called in memory of his ancestor "my Rosinante." He couldn't bear the thought of his little car rusting in a scrap heap. He had sometimes thought of buying a small plot of land and leaving it as an inheritance to one of his parishioners on condition that a sheltered corner be reserved for his car to rest in, but there was not one parishioner whom he could trust to carry out his wish, and in any case a slow death of rust could not be avoided and perhaps a crusher of a steelworks would be a more merciful end. Thinking of all this for the hundredth time he nearly ran into a stationary black Mercedes which was parked round the corner on the main road. He assumed that the dark clothed figure at the wheel was taking a rest on the long drive from Valencia to Madrid, and he went on to buy his jar of wine at the collective without pausing; it was only as he returned that he became aware of a white Roman collar, like a handkerchief signalling distress. How on earth, he wondered, could one of his brother priests afford a Mercedes? But when he drew up he noticed a scarlet bib below the collar which denoted at least a monsignor if not a bishop.

Father Quixote had reason to be afraid of bishops; he was well aware how much his own Bishop, who regarded him in spite of his distinguished ancestry as little better than a peasant, disliked him. "How can he be descended from a fictional character?" he had demanded in a private conversation which had been promptly reported to Father Quixote.

The man to whom the Bishop had spoken asked with surprise: "A *fictional* character?"

"A character in a novel by an overrated writer called Cervantes— a novel moreover with many disgusting passages which in the days of the Generalissimo would not even have passed the censor."

"But, your Grace, you can see the house of Dulcinea in El Toboso. There it is marked on a plaque; the house of Dulcinea."

"A trap for tourists. Why," the Bishop went on with asperity, "Quixote is not even a Spanish patronymic. Cervantes himself says the surname was probably Quixada or Quesada or even Quexana, and on his deathbed Quixote calls himself Quixano."

"I can see that you have read the book then your Grace."

"I have never got beyond the first chapter. Although of course I have glanced at the last. My usual habit with novels."

"Perhaps some ancestor of the Father was called Quixada or Quexana."

"Men of that class have no ancestors."

It was with trepidation then that Father Quixote introduced himself to the high clerical figure in the distinguished Mercedes. "My name is Padre Quixote, Monsignor. Can I be of any service?"

"You certainly can, my friend. I am the Bishop of Motopo"—he spoke with a strong Italian accent.

"Bishop of Motopo?"

"*In partibus infidelium*, my friend. Is there a garage near here? My car refuses to go on any further, and if there should be a restaurant—

my stomach begins to clamour for food."

"There is a garage in my village, but it is closed because of a funeral—the mother-in-law of the garagist has died."

"May she rest in peace," the Bishop said automatically, clutching at his pectoral cross. He added, "What a confounded nuisance."

"He'll be back in a few hours."

"A few hours! Is there a restaurant anywhere near?"

"Monsignor, if you would honour me by sharing my humble lunch ... the restaurant in El Toboso is not to be recommended, neither for the food nor for the wine."

"A glass of wine is essential in my situation."

"I can offer you a good little local wine and if you would be contented with a simple steak ... and a salad. My housekeeper always prepares more than I can eat ..."

"My friend, you certainly prove to be my guardian angel in disguise. Let us go."

The front seat of the little Fiat was occupied by the jar of wine, but the Bishop insisted on crouching—he was a very tall man—in the back. "We cannot disturb the wine," he said.

"It is not an important wine, Monsignor, and you will be much more comfortable ..."

"No wine can be regarded as unimportant, my friend, since the marriage at Cana."

Father Quixote felt rebuked and silence fell between them until they arrived at his small house near the church. He was much relieved when the Bishop, who had to stoop to enter the door which led directly into the priest's parlour, remarked, "It is an honour for me to be a guest in the house of Don Quixote."

"My Bishop does not approve of the book."

"Holiness and literary appreciation don't always go together."

The Bishop went to the bookshelf where Father Quixote kept

his missal, his breviary, the New Testament and a few tattered volumes of a theological kind, the relics of his studies.

"If you will excuse me, Monsignor ..."

Father Quixote went to find his housekeeper in the kitchen which served also as her bedroom and it must be admitted the kitchen sink was her only washbasin. She was a square woman with protruding teeth and an embryo moustache; she trusted no one living, but had a certain regard for the saints, the female ones. Her name was Teresa, and no one in El Toboso had nicknamed her Dulcinea, since no one but the Mayor, who was reputed to be Communist, had read Cervantes' work, and it was doubtful if he had got further than the battle with the windmills.

"Teresa," Don Quixote said, "we have a guest for lunch which must be prepared quickly."

"There is only your steak and a salad, and what remains of the manchego cheese."

"My steak is always big enough for two, and the Bishop is an amiable man."

"The Bishop? I won't serve him."

"Not *our* Bishop. An Italian. A very courteous man."

He explained the situation in which he had found the Bishop.

"But the steak ..." Teresa said.

"What about the steak?"

"You can't give the Bishop horse meat."

"My steak is horse meat?"

"It always has been. How can I give you beef with the money you allow me?"

"You have nothing else?"

"Nothing."

"Oh dear, oh dear. We can only pray that he doesn't notice. After all, I have never noticed."

"*You* have never eaten anything better."

Father Quixote returned to the Bishop in a troubled state of mind, carrying with him a half bottle of Marsala. He was glad when the Bishop accepted a glass and then a second one. Perhaps the drink might confuse his taste buds. He had settled himself deeply in Father Quixote's only easy chair. Father Quixote watched him with anxiety. The Bishop didn't look dangerous. He had a very smooth face which might never have known a razor. Father Quixote regretted that he had neglected to shave that morning after early Mass which he had celebrated in an empty church.

"You're on holiday, Monsignor?"

"Not exactly on holiday, though it is true I am enjoying my change from Rome. The Holy Father has entrusted me with a little confidential mission because of my knowledge of Spanish. I suppose, Father, that you see a great many foreign tourists in El Toboso."

"Not many, Monsignor, for there is very little for them to see here, except for the Museum."

"What do you keep in the Museum?"

"It is a very small Museum, Monsignor, one room. No bigger than my parlour. It holds nothing of interest except the signatures."

"What do you mean by the signatures? May I perhaps have another glass of Marsala? Sitting in the sun in that broken-down car has made me very thirsty."

"Forgive me, Monsignor. You see how unused I am to being a host."

"I have never encountered before a Museum of Signatures."

"You see the Mayor of El Toboso years ago began writing to Heads of State asking for translations of Cervantes with a signature. The collection is quite remarkable. Of course there is General Franco's signature in what I would call the master copy, and there is Mussolini's and Hitler's (very tiny his, like a fly's mess) and

Churchill's and Hindenburg's and someone called Ramsay MacDonald—I suppose he was the Prime Minister of Scotland."

"Of England, Father."

Teresa came in with the steaks and they seated themselves at table and the Bishop said grace.

Father Quixote poured out the wine and watched with apprehension as the Bishop took his first slice of steak, which he quickly washed down with wine—perhaps to take away the taste.

"It is a very common wine, Monsignor, but here we are very proud of what we call the manchegan."

"The wine is agreeable," the Bishop said, "but the steak ... the steak," he said, staring at his plate while Father Quixote waited for the worst, "the steak ... " he said a third time as though he were seeking in his memory of ancient rites for the correct term of anathema—Teresa meanwhile hovered in the doorway waiting too— "never, at any table, have I tasted ... so tender, so flavoursome, I am tempted to be blasphemous and say so divine a steak. I would like to congratulate your admirable housekeeper."

"She is here, Monsignor."

"My dear lady, let me shake your hand."

The Bishop held out his beringed hand palm down as though he expected a kiss rather than a shake. Teresa backed hurriedly into the kitchen. "Did I say something wrong?" the Bishop asked.

"No, no, Monsignor. It is only that she is unaccustomed to cooking for a Bishop."

"She has a plain and honest face. In these days one is often embarrassed to find even in Italy very *marriageable* housekeepers— and alas! only too often marriage does follow."

Teresa came rapidly in with some cheese and retired at the same speed.

"A little of our *queso manchego*, Monsignor?"

"And perhaps another glass of wine to go with it?

Father Quixote began to feel warm and comfortable. He was encouraged to press a question which he wouldn't have dared to ask his own Bishop. A Roman Bishop after all was closer to the fount of faith, and the Bishop's welcome to the steak of horsemeat encouraged him. It was not for nothing that he had called his Fiat Five Rosinante, and he was more likely to receive a favourable answer if he spoke of her as a horse.

"Monsignor," he said, "there is one question I have often asked myself, a question which is perhaps likely to occur more frequently to a countryman than to a city dweller." He hesitated like a swimmer on a cold brink. "Would you consider it heretical to pray to God for the life of a horse?"

"For the terrestrial life," the Bishop answered without hesitation, "no—a prayer would be perfectly allowable. The Fathers teach us that God created animals for man's use, and a long life of service for a horse is as desirable in the eyes of God as a long life for my Mercedes which I am afraid looks like failing me. I must admit, however, that there is no record of miracles in the case of inanimate objects, but in the case of beasts we have the example of Balaam's ass who by the mercy of God proved of more than usual use to Balaam."

"I was thinking less of the use of a horse to its master than a prayer for its happiness—and even for a good death."

"I see no objection to praying for its happiness—it might well make it docile and of greater use to its owner, but I am not sure what you mean by a good death in the case of a horse. A good death for a man means a death in communion with God, a promise of eternity. We may pray for the terrestrial life of a horse, but not for its eternal life—that would surely be verging on heresy. It is true there is a movement in the Church which would grant the possibility that a dog may have what one may call an embryo soul, though personally I find the idea sentimental and dangerous. We mustn't open unnecessary doors by imprudent speculation. If a dog has a soul, why not a rhinoceros or a kangaroo?"

"Or a mosquito?"

"Exactly. I can see, Father, that you are on the right side."

"But I have never understood, Monsignor, how a mosquito could have been created for man's use. What use?"

"Surely, Father, the use is obvious. A mosquito may be likened to a scourge in the hands of God. It teaches us to endure pain for love of him. That painful buzz in the ear—perhaps it is God buzzing."

Father Quixote had the unfortunate habit of a lonely man: he spoke his thoughts aloud. "The same would apply to a flea." The Bishop eyed him closely, but there was no sign of humour in Father Quixote's gaze: it was obvious that he had plunged deeply in his own thoughts.

"These are great mysteries," the Bishop told him. "Where would our faith be if there were no mysteries?"

"I am wondering," Father Quixote said, "where I have put the bottle of cognac that a man from Tomelloso brought me some three years back. This might be the right moment for opening it. If you will excuse me, Monsignor ... Teresa may know." He made for the kitchen.

"He has drunk quite enough for a Bishop," Teresa said.

"Hush! Your voice carries. The poor Bishop is very worried about his car. He feels it has failed him."

"In my opinion, it is all his own fault. When I was a girl I lived in Africa. Negroes and bishops always forget to refill with petrol."

"You really think ... It's true he is a very unworldly man. He believes that the buzz of a mosquito ... Teresa, take him in the cognac and tell him I have gone to see if I can arrange about his car."

He took a jerrycan of petrol in the boot of Rosinante. He didn't

believe the problem was as simple as all that, but there was no harm
in trying, and sure enough the gauge showed that the tank was empty.
Why hadn't the Bishop noticed? Perhaps he had and was too ashamed
to admit his foolishness to a country priest. He felt sorry for the
Bishop. Unlike his own Bishop, the Italian was a kind man. He had
drunk the young wine without complaint, he had eaten the horse
steak with relish. Father Quixote didn't want to humiliate him. But
how was he to save the Bishop's face? He ruminated for a long time
against the bonnet of the Mercedes. If the Bishop has not noticed the
gauge it would be easy to pretend a mechanical knowledge which he
didn't possess, but how was he to know? In any case it would be as
well to get some oil on his hands ...

The Bishop was quite happy with the cognac from Tomelloso.
He had found on the shelves among the textbooks a copy of
Cervantes' work which Father Quixote had bought when he was a
boy, and he was smiling over a page as his own Bishop would certainly
not have done.

"Here is a very apposite passage, Father, which I was reading as
you came in. What a moral writer Cervantes was whatever your
Bishop may say. 'It is the duty of loyal vassals to tell their lords the
truth in its proper shape and essence without enlarging on it out of
flattery or softening it for any idle reason. I would have you know,
Sancho, that if the naked truth were to come to the ears of princes,
unclothed in flattery, this would be a different age.' In what condition
did you find the Mercedes, has it been bewitched by some sorcerer in
this dangerous region of La Mancha?"

"The Mercedes is ready to be driven, Monsignor."

"A miracle? Or has the garagist returned from the funeral?"

"The garagist has not yet returned, so I took a look at the engine
myself." He held out his hands. "A messy job. You were very low in
petrol—that was easy to remedy—I always have a spare jerrycan, but

what was the real fault?"

"Ah, it wasn't only the petrol," the Bishop said with satisfaction.

"There were some adjustments to be made to the engine—I never know the technical names for these things—it needed a good deal of fiddling around, but it is working satisfactorily now. Perhaps when you reach Madrid, Monsignor, it would be as well to get a professional overhaul."

"Then I can be off?"

"Unless you would like to have a short siesta. Teresa could prepare my bed."

"No, no, Father. I feel completely refreshed by your excellent wine and the steak—ah the steak. Besides, I have a dinner tonight in Madrid and I don't like driving in the dark."

As they made their way to the main road the Bishop questioned Father Quixote. "For how many years have you lived in El Toboso, Father?"

"Since my birth, Monsignor. Except during my studies for the priesthood."

"Where did you study?"

"In Madrid. I would have preferred Salamanca, but the standard there was beyond me."

"A man of your ability is wasted in El Toboso. Surely your Bishop ..."

"My Bishop, alas, knows how small my abilities are."

"Could your Bishop have mended my car?"

"My spiritual abilities I meant."

"In the Church we have need of men of practical abilities too. In the world of today *astucia*—in the sense of worldly wisdom—must be allied to prayer. A priest who can set before an unexpected guest good wine, good cheese and a remarkable steak is a priest who can hold his own in the highest circles. We are here to bring sinners to repentance and there are more sinners among the bourgeois than among peasants. I would like you to go forth like your ancestor Don Quixote on the highroads of the world ..."

"He was a madman, Monsignor."

"So many said of St Ignatius. But here is one high road I have to take and here is my Mercedes ..."

"He was a fiction, my Bishop says, in the mind of a writer ..."

"Perhaps we are all fictions, Father, in the mind of God."

"Do you want me to tilt at windmills?"

"It was only by tilting at windmills that Don Quixote found the truth on his deathbed," the Bishop seating himself at the wheel of the Mercedes intoned in Gregorian accents, "' there are no birds this year in last year's nests'."

"It's a beautiful phrase," Father Quixote said, "but what did he mean by it?"

"I have never quite made it out myself," the Bishop replied, "but surely the beauty is enough," and as the Mercedes purred with gentle health on the road towards Madrid, Father Quixote realised with his nose that the Bishop had left behind him for a brief instant an agreeable smell compounded of young wine, of cognac, and of manchegan cheese which before it dispersed a stranger might well have mistaken for an exotic incense.

Many weeks passed with all the comforting unbroken rhythms of former years. Now that Father Quixote knew that his occasional steak consisted of horse meat he would greet it with an unguilty smile—no need to reproach himself for luxury—in memory of the Italian Bishop who had shown such kindness, such courtesy, such love of wine. It seemed to him that one of the pagan gods he had read about in his Latin studies had rested for an hour or two under his roof-tree. He read very little now except his breviary and the newspaper, which had never informed him that the breviary was no longer required reading;

he was interested particularly in the accounts of the cosmonauts since he had never quite been able to abandon the idea that somewhere in the immensity of space existed the realm of God—and occasionally he would open one of his old theological textbooks to make sure that the short homily which he would be making in the church on Sundays was properly in accordance with the teaching of the Church.

He also received once a month from Madrid a theological magazine. There were criticisms in it referring sometimes to dangerous ideas—spoken even by a cardinal, in Holland or Belgium, he forgot which—or written by a priest who had a Teutonic name which made him remember Luther—but he paid little attention to such criticisms, for it was very unlikely that he would have to defend the orthodoxy of the Church against the butcher, the baker or the garagist, who were the most educated men in El Toboso except for the Mayor, and as he was suspected by the Bishop to be an atheist and a secret Communist, he could safely be ignored as far as the doctrine of the Church was concerned. Indeed he enjoyed the Mayor's company for a street corner chat more than that of his parishioners. In the company of the Mayor, whose name was Sancho Martinez, he ceased to feel himself a kind of official superior; they had the equality of a common interest in the progress through space of the cosmonauts, and they were tactful with each other. Father Quixote did not speak of the possibility of an encounter between a sputnik and the angelic host and the Mayor showed a scientific impartiality between the Russian and the American achievements, not that Father Quixote saw much difference between the crews from a Christian point of view—both crews seemed to him to consist of good people, probably good parents and good husbands, but in their helmets and space suits, which might well have been provided by the same haberdasher, he couldn't imagine either of them in the company of Gabriel or Michael, and certainly not of Lucifer, if instead of rising to the realm of God their spaceship should take a headlong spin towards the infernal regions.

"You've got a letter," Teresa told him with suspicion. "I didn't know where to find you."

"I was up the street talking to the Mayor."

"That heretic."

"If there were no heretics, Teresa, there would be little for a priest to do."

She snarled at him, "It's a letter from the Bishop."

"Oh dear, oh dear." He sat with it for a long time in his hand, fearing to open it. He couldn't remember a single letter from his Bishop which hadn't included a complaint of one kind or another. There had been, for example, the time when he had diverted the Easter offering which traditionally belonged in his own pocket to the pocket of a representative of a charity with the worthy Latin name of *In Vinculis*, purporting to look after the spiritual needs of poor imprisoned men. It was a private act of benevolence which had somehow reached the Bishop's ears after the collector had been arrested for organising the escape of certain incarcerated enemies of the Generalissimo. The Bishop had called him a fool—a term which Christ had deprecated. The Mayor on the other hand had clapped him on the back and called him a worthy descendant of his great ancestor who had released the galley slaves. And then there was the time ... and that other time ... he would have given himself a glass of Marsala to give him courage had he had any left after entertaining the Bishop of Motopo.

With a sigh he broke the red seal and opened the envelope. As he had feared the letter had been written in a cold rage. "I have received an utterly incomprehensible letter from Rome," the Bishop wrote, "which at first I took for a joke in the worst of taste imitating an ecclesiastical style and possibly inspired by a member of that

Communist organisation which you thought it your duty to support from motives which have always been obscure to me. But on asking for confirmation I have today received an abrupt letter confirming the first missive and asking me at once to communicate to you that the Holy Father has seen fit—for what strange stirring of the Holy Spirit it is not for me to enquire—to promote you to the rank of monsignor, apparently on the recommendation of a Bishop of Motopo, of whom I have never heard, without any reference to me, through whom such a recommendation should naturally have come—a most unlikely action on my part, I need hardly add. I have obeyed the Holy Father in passing on the news to you, and I can only pray that you will not disgrace the title he has seen fit to grant you. Certain scandals which were only forgiven because they originated in the ignorance of the parish priest of El Toboso would have far greater resonance if caused by the imprudence of Monsignor Quixote. So prudence, my dear Father, prudence I beg of you. I have written to Rome, however, pointing out the absurdity of a small parish like El Toboso being in the hands of a monsignor, a title which will be resented by many deserving priests in La Mancha and asking for aid in finding wider scope for your activities, perhaps in another diocese or even in the mission field."

He closed the letter and it dropped to the floor. "What does he say?" Teresa asked.

"He wants to drive me away from El Toboso," Father Quixote said in a tone of such despair that Teresa went quickly back into the kitchen to hide from his sad eyes.

20/27 December 1980

Reading for Christmas

HOW MONSIGNOR QUIXOTE SET OFF ON HIS TRAVELS

"Here is part of the next chapter of *Monsignor Quixote*", Greene wrote to Burns on 15th November 1980. "It has much less action than the earlier piece and you may not feel that is stands alone as the other did. I shan't be offended in that case." The extract was nevertheless published in its entirety and, fortunately for Burns, this time Greene was satisfied with the result. "The Christmas number [of *The Tablet*] is very elegant and the little drawings this time are completely inoffensive."

Tablet notice:

In our Christmas issue of 1978 we published a piece of work in progress which Graham Greene said might never be completed. It was called "How Fr Quixote became a Monsignor." The work has in fact progressed since then, and what follows are two further sections of it. For readers who missed the first instalment we give a brief summary.

Fr Quixote, the parish priest of El Toboso, is driving his aged little Fiat—which he calls Rosinante after his famous forebear's horse—when he comes across a stationary Mercedes on the main Madrid-Valencia road. It has apparently broken down and the driver, who turns out to be a bishop, is in deep distress. Fr Quixote invites him to his home nearby, offering, as he says, a humble meal, and the bishop accepts. He is delighted with the steak and salad and wine which Fr Quixote's housekeeper provides, saying that the steak is the most succulent he has ever tasted. What he does not realise is that the steak was horsemeat; Fr Quixote could not afford anything better. Having fed him, Fr Quixote leaves the bishop comfortably installed and takes a jerrycan of petrol to the marooned Mercedes and his suspicion that it had simply run out of petrol is justified; but the good priest, not to embarrass the bishop returns with soiled hands and talk of minor necessary adjustments which he has duly carried out. He reports that the car is ready for the road. The bishop departs, full of gratitude. Earlier he had explained that he was a curial bishop from Rome and would be returning there shortly.

The climax of the story comes when Fr Quixote receives a letter from his own bishop (they are on very cool terms) telling him that for some inexplicable reason Rome had decided to promote him to the rank of monsignor. This, says his bishop, means that he must move from El Toboso, where his superior rank might produce difficulties with his neighbouring parish priests, and find a wider scope for his activities. Fr Quixote tells his tearful housekeeper that this is a hard blow as he had no wish to leave his beloved parish. His round of goodbye visits includes one to the former mayor of the village, a Communist with whom he had been on friendly terms.

It happened a week after the Bishop's letter had been delivered to Father Quixote that local elections were held in the province of La Mancha and the Mayor of El Toboso suffered an unexpected defeat. "The forces of the Right," he told Father Quixote, "have re-formed, they seek another Generalissimo," and he spoke of certain intrigues of which he was well informed between the garagist, the butcher and the owner of a second-rate restaurant, who, it seemed, wanted to enlarge his premises. Money, he said, had been lent to the landlord by a mysterious stranger and he had bought a new deep freeze. In some way which Father Quixote was unable to fathom, this had seriously affected the election results.

"I wash my hands of El Toboso," the ex-Mayor said.

"And I am being driven away by the Bishop," Father Quixote confided, and he told his melancholy story.

"I could have warned you. This comes of putting your trust in the Church."

"It is not a question of the Church but a Bishop. I have never cared for the Bishop, may God forgive me. But you, I am deeply sorry for you, my friend. You have been let down by your Party, Sancho."

The Mayor's name was Zancas, which was the name of the original Sancho Panza in Cervantes' truthful history, and though his Christian name was Enrique he permitted his friend Father Quixote to tease him with the name of Sancho.

"It is not a question of my Party. Three men alone have done this to me," and he mentioned again the butcher, the garagist and the affair of the deep freeze. "There are traitors in every Party. In your Party too, Father Quixote. There was Judas ..."

"And in yours there was Stalin."

"Don't bring up that old stale history now."

"The history of Judas is even older."

"Alexander the VI ..."

"Trotsky. Though I suppose you may be allowed now to have a difference of opinion about Trotsky." There was little logic in their argument, but it was the nearest they had ever come to a quarrel.

"And what about your opinion of Judas? He's a saint in the Ethiopian Church."

"Sancho, Sancho, we disagree too profoundly to dispute. Let us go to my house and have a glass of cognac ... Oh, I forgot, the Bishop finished the bottle."

"The Bishop ... You allowed that scoundrel ..."

"It was a different bishop. A good man, the cause of my trouble all the same."

"You had better come to my house then and have a glass of honest vodka."

"Vodka?"

"Polish vodka, Father, from a Catholic country."

It was the first time Father Quixote had tasted vodka. The first glass seemed to him to lack flavour—the second gave him a sense of exhilaration. He said, "You will miss your duties as a mayor, Sancho."

"I plan to take a holiday. I have not stepped out of El Toboso for five years. If only I had a car ..."

Father Quixote thought of Rosinante and his mind wandered.

"Moscow is too far," the voice of the Mayor went on. "Besides it is too cold. East Germany ... I have no desire to go there, we have seen too many Germans in Spain."

Suppose, Father Quixote thought, I am expelled to Rome. Rosinante could never make so great a distance. The Bishop had even spoken of a mission field. Rosinante was near the end of her days. He couldn't leave her to die by some roadside in Africa to be cannibalised for the sake of a gear-box or a door handle.

"San Marino is the nearest state where the Party rules. Another glass, Father."

Without thinking, Father Quixote extended his hand.

"What will you do, Father, away from El Toboso?"

"I shall obey orders. I will go where I am sent."

"To preach to the converted as you do here?"

"That is an easy sneer, Sancho. I doubt if anyone is ever fully converted."

"Not even the Pope?"

"Perhaps, poor man, not even the Pope. Who knows what he thinks at night in his bed when he has said his prayers?"

"And you?"

"Oh, I am as ignorant as anyone in the parish. I have read more books, that is all, when I studied, but one forgets ..."

"All the same you do believe all that nonsense. God, the Trinity, the Immaculate Conception..."

"I *want* to believe. And I want others to believe."

"Why?"

"I want them to be happy."

"Let them drink a little vodka then. That's better than a make-believe."

"The vodka wears off. It's wearing off even now."

"So does belief."

Father Quixote looked up with surprise. He had been gazing with a certain wistfulness at the last drops in his glass.

"Your belief?"

"And your belief."

"Why do you think that?"

"It's life, Father, at its dirty work. Belief dies away like desire for a woman. I doubt if you are an exception to the general rule."

"Do you think it would be bad for me to have another glass?"

"Vodka has never done anyone any harm."

"I was astonished the other day at how much the Bishop of Motopo drank."

"Where is Motopo?"

"*In partibus infidelium.*"

"I've long ago forgotten the little Latin I once had."

"I didn't know you ever had any."

"My parents wanted me to be a priest. I have never told you that before, Father. *In vodka veritas.*"

"So that was how you knew about the Ethiopian Church? I was a little surprised."

"There are small bits of useless knowledge which stick to one's brain like barnacles to a boat. By the way you have read how the Soviet cosmonauts have beaten the endurance record in outer space?"

"I heard something of the sort on the radio yesterday."

"Yet in all that time they haven't encountered a single angel."

"Have you read, Sancho, about the black holes in space?"

"I know what you are going to say, Father. But the word holes is used only in a metaphoric sense. One more glass. Don't be afraid of any bishop."

"Your vodka inspires me with hope."

"Of what?"

"A forlorn hope you would say."

"Go on. Tell me. What hope?"

"I can't tell you. You would laugh at me. One day perhaps I will tell you of my hope. If God grant me the time. And you the time too of course."

"We should see more of each other, Father. Perhaps I will convert you to Marx."

"You have a Marx on your shelves?"

"Of course."

"*Das Kapital?*"

"Yes. Among others. There it is. I haven't read any of it for a long time. To tell you the truth I've always found parts ... Well, remote ... All the statistics about the English industrial revolution. I imagine you find parts of the Bible dull too."

"Thank God, we are not expected to study Numbers or Deuteronomy, but the Gospels are not dull. My goodness, look at the time. Is it vodka that makes time go so fast?"

"You know, Father, you remind me of your ancestor. He believed in all those books of chivalry, quite out of date even in his day ..."

"I've never read a book of chivalry in my life."

"But you continue to read those old books of theology. They are your books of chivalry. You believe in them just as much as he did in his books."

"But the voice of the Church doesn't date, Sancho."

"Oh yes, Father, it does. Your second Vatican Council put even St John out of date."

"What nonsense you talk."

"No longer at the end of Mass do you read those words of St John—'He was in the world and the world was made by Him and the world knew Him not.'"

"How strange that you should know that."

"Oh, I've sometimes come in at the end of Mass—to make sure none of my people are there."

"I still say those words."

"But you don't say them aloud. Your Bishop wouldn't allow it. You are like your ancestor who read his books of chivalry secretly so that only his niece and his doctor knew until … "

"What a lot of nonsense you talk, Sancho."

"Until he broke away on Rosinante to do his deeds of chivalry in a world that didn't believe in those old stories."

"Accompanied by an ignorant man called Sancho," Father Quixote replied with a touch of anger which he immediately regretted.

"Accompanied by Sancho," the Mayor repeated. "Why not?"

"The Bishop could hardly deny me a short holiday."

"You must go to Madrid to buy your uniform."

"Uniform? What uniform?"

"Purple socks, Monsignor, and a purple—what do you call that thing you wear below the collar?"

"A *pechera*. That's rubbish. Nobody will make me wear purple socks and a purple …"

"You're in the army of the Church, Father. You can't refuse the badges of rank."

"I never asked to be a monsignor."

"Of course you could retire from the army altogether."

"Could you retire from the Party?"

Each took another glass of vodka and fell into a comradely silence, a silence in which dreams had room to grow.

"Do you think your car could get us as far as Moscow?"

"Rosinante is too old for that. She'd break down on the way. Anyway the Bishop would not consider Moscow suitable for a holiday."

"You are no longer the Bishop's servant, Monsignor."

"But the Holy Father ... You know Rosinante might perhaps get as far as Rome."

"I don't fancy Rome at all."

"Rome has a Communist mayor, Sancho."

"I don't fancy a Euro-Communist any more than you fancy a Protestant. What's the matter, Father? You are upset about something."

"The vodka gave me a dream, and another vodka has taken it away."

"Don't worry. You aren't used to vodka and it has gone to your head."

"Why such a happy dream ... and afterwards despair?"

"I know what you mean. Vodka sometimes has that effect on me, if I take a little too much. I'll see you home, Father."

At Father Quixote's door they parted.

"Go and lie down for a little."

"Teresa would find it rather odd at this hour. And I haven't yet read my breviary."

"That's no longer compulsory."

"I find it hard to break a habit. Habits can be comforting, even rather boring habits."

"Yes. I think I understand. There are even times when I dip into *The Communist Manifesto*."

"Does it comfort you?"

"Sometimes—a little, not very much. But a little."

"You must lend it to me. One day."

"Perhaps on our travels."

"You still believe in our travels? I doubt very much whether we are the right companions, you and I. A big gulf separates us, Sancho."

"A big gulf separated your ancestor from the one you call mine,

Father, and yet ..."

"Yes. And yet ... " Father Quixote turned hurriedly away. He went into his study and took his breviary from the shelf, but before reading more than a few sentences, he fell asleep, and all that he could remember when he woke was that he had climbed a high tree and dislodged a nest, empty and dry and brittle, the relic of a year gone by.

✳ ✳ ✳

It needed a great deal of courage for Father Quixote to write to the Bishop and an even greater courage to open the letter received in reply after some days. It began abruptly "Monsignor"—the sound of the title was like acid on the tongue. "El Toboso," the Bishop wrote, "is one of the smallest parishes in my diocese, and I cannot believe that the burden of your duties has been a very heavy one. However I am ready to grant your request for a period of repose and I am despatching a young priest Father Herreira to look after El Toboso in your absence. I trust you will delay your holiday until you are fully satisfied that Father Herreira is aware of all the problems that may exist in your parish, so that you can leave your people with complete confidence in his care. The defeat of the Mayor of El Toboso in the recent election seems to indicate that the tide is turning at last in the proper direction and perhaps a younger priest with the shrewdness and discretion of Father Herreira (he won golden opinions as well as a doctorate in moral theology at Salamanca) will be better able to take advantage of the current than an older man. As you will guess I have written to the Archbishop with regard to your future, and I have small doubt that by the time you return from your holiday we will have found you a sphere of action more suitable than El Toboso and carrying a lesser burden of duties for a priest of your age and rank." It was an even worse letter than Father Quixote had expected, and he waited anxiously for the arrival of Father Herreira. He told Teresa that Father Herreira would take immediate possession of his bedroom and asked her to find if it were possible a folding camp bed for the living-room. "If you cannot find one," he said, "the armchair is quite comfortable for me. I have slept in it often in the afternoon."

"If he's young let him sleep in the armchair."

"For the time being he is my guest, Teresa."

"What do you mean—for the time being?"

"I think the Bishop is likely to make him my successor. I am getting old, Teresa."

"If you are that old, you shouldn't go gallivanting off—the good God alone knows where. Anyway don't expect me to work for another priest."

"Give him a chance, Teresa, give him a chance. But don't on any account tell him the secret of your admirable horse steaks."

Three days passed and Father Herreira arrived. Father Quixote who had gone to have a chat with the ex-Mayor found the young priest on the doorstep carrying a smart suitcase. Teresa was barring his entrance, a kitchen cloth in her hand. Father Herreira was perhaps naturally pale, but he looked agitated and the sun gleamed on his clerical collar. "Monsignor Quixote?" he asked. "I am Father Herreira. This woman won't let me in."

"Teresa, Teresa, this is very unkind of you. Where are your manners? This is our guest. Go and get Father Herreira a cup of coffee."

"No. Please not. I never drink coffee. It keeps me awake at night."

In the sitting-room Father Herreira took the only armchair without hesitation.

"What a very violent woman," he said. "I told her that I was sent by the Bishop and she said something very rude."

"Like all of us, she has her prejudices."

"The Bishop would *not* have been pleased."

"Well he didn't hear her, and we won't tell him, will we?"

"I was quite shocked, Monsignor."

"I wish you wouldn't call me Monsignor. Call me Father if you like. I'm old enough to be your father. Have you experience of parish work?"

"Not directly. I've been his Lordship's secretary for three years. Since I left Salamanca."

"You may find it difficult at first. There are many Teresas in El Toboso. But I am sure you will learn very quickly. Your doctorate was in ... let me remember?"

"Moral theology."

"Ah, I always found that a very difficult subject. I very nearly failed to pass—even in Madrid."

"I see you have Heribert Jone on your shelf. A German. All the same very sound."

"I am afraid I haven't read him for many years. Moral theology, as you can imagine, doesn't play a great part in parish work."

"I would have thought it essential, in the confessional."

"When the baker comes—or the garagist—it's not very often— their problems are usually very simple ones. Well, I trust to my instinct. There's no time to look their problems up in Jone."

"Instinct must have a sound basis, Monsignor—Father, I mean."

"Oh yes, of course, a sound basis. Yes. But like my ancestor, perhaps I put my trust most in old books written before Jone was born."

"But your ancestor's books were only of chivalry surely."

"Well, perhaps mine—in their way—are too. St John of the Cross,

St Teresa, St Francis de Sales. And the Gospels, Father. 'Let us go up to Jerusalem and die with him.' Don Quixote could not have put it better."

"Oh, of course, the Gospels, naturally," Father Herreira said in the tone of one who surrenders a small and unimportant point to his adversary. "All the same Jone on moral theology is very sound, very sound. What's that you said, Father?"

"Oh, nothing. A truism which I haven't the right to use. I was going to add another sound base is God's love."

"Of course, of course. But we mustn't forget his justice either. You agree, Monsignor?"

"Yes, well, I suppose."

"Jone makes a very clear distinction between love and justice."

"Did you take a secretarial course, Father? After Salamanca, I mean."

"Certainly. I can type and without boasting I can claim to be very good at shorthand."

Teresa put her head round the door. "Will you have a steak for lunch, Father?"

"Two steaks, please Teresa."

The sunlight flashed again on Father Herriera's collar as he turned: the flash was like a helio signal sending what message? Father Quixote thought he had never before seen so clean a collar or indeed so clean a man. You would have thought, so smooth and white was his skin, that it had never needed a razor. That comes from living so long in El Toboso, he thought, I am a rough countryman. I live very, very far away from Salamanca.

The day of departure came at last. Rosinante had been passed by the garagist, though rather grudgingly, as fit to leave. "I can guarantee nothing," he said. "You should have turned her in five years ago. All the same she ought to get you as far as Madrid."

"And back again I hope," Father Quixote said.

"That is another matter."

The Mayor could hardly contain his impatience to be gone. He had no desire to see his successor installed. "A black Fascist. We are back in the days of Franco."

"God rest his soul," Father Quixote added with a certain automatism.

"He had no soul."

Their luggage filled the book and the back seat was given up to four cases of honest Manchegan wine. "You can't trust the wine in Madrid", the Mayor said. "This is at least an honest co-operative."

"Why should we go to Madrid?" Father Quixote asked. "I disliked the city a great deal when I was a student and I have never been back. Why not take the road to Cuenca? Cuenca, I am told, is a beautiful town and a great deal nearer to El Toboso. I don't want to overtire Rosinante."

"You cannot buy purple socks in Cuenca."

"Those purple socks! I refuse to buy purple socks. I can't afford to waste money on purple socks, Sancho."

"Your ancestor had a proper respect for the uniform of a knight errant, even though he had to put up with a barber's basin for a helmet. You are a Monsignor errant and you must wear purple socks."

"They say my ancestor was mad. They will say the same of me. I will be brought back in disgrace. Indeed I must be a little mad, for I am mocked with the title of Monsignor and I am leaving El Toboso in charge of that young priest."

"The baker has a poor opinion of him and I've seen him myself in close talk with that reactionary of the restaurant."

Father Quixote insisted on taking the wheel. "Rosinante has certain tricks of her own which only I know."

"You are taking the wrong road."

"I have to go to the house once more, I have forgotten something."

He left the Mayor in the car. The young priest, he knew, was at church. He wanted to be alone for the last time in the house where he had lived for more than thirty years. Besides he had forgotten Father Heribert Jone's work on moral theology. St John of the Cross was in the boot and so was St Teresa and St Francis de Sales. He had a little unwillingly promised Father Herreira to balance these old books with a more modern work of theology which he had not opened since the days when he was a student. "Instinct must have a sound basis," Father Herreira had correctly said. If the Mayor began to quote Marx to him Father Heribert Jone might prove useful in reply. Anyway it was a small book which fitted easily into a pocket. He sat down for a few moments in his arm chair. The seat had been shaped by his body through the years and its shape was as familiar to him as the curve of the saddle must have been to his ancestor. He could hear Teresa move pans in the kitchen, keeping up the angry mutter which had been the music of his morning solitude. I will miss even her ill humour, he thought. Outside the Mayor impatiently sounded the horn.

"I'm sorry to have kept you waiting," Father Quixote said, and Rosinante gave a deep groan as he changed gear.

They said very little to each other. It was as though the strangeness of their adventure weighed on their spirits. Once the Mayor spoke his thought aloud. "We must have something in common, Father, or why do you go with me?"

"I suppose—friendship?"

"Is that enough?"

"We will find out in time."

More than an hour passed in silence. Then the Mayor spoke again, "What is upsetting you, friend?"

"We have just left La Mancha—nothing seems safe any more."

"Not even your faith?"

It was a question Father Quixote did not bother to answer.

19/26 December 1981

Reading For Christmas

A VISIT FROM THE BISHOP

On 10th October 1981, Greene wrote to Burns to say the
Quixote saga had temporarily stalled. "I am afraid I can't let
you have another instalment for the Christmas number
because I am too immersed in the final stages and there is no
single episode which I would want to see appear separate from
the rest." However, Burns implored Greene for just one more
episode to mark his departure from *The Tablet* as editor after the
Christmas 1981 issue; Greene generously rounded off the saga.
Four years later, in 1985, Greene wrote again to Burns to say
that *Monsignor Quixote* was about to be made into a television
film starring Alec Guinness. "I haven't done the script but I
have supervised it to some extent—in fact a small extent
because I found the script by [Christopher] Neame an
admirable one and very close to the book. He toured the whole
of the route of Monsignor Quixote with Leopoldo Durán and
they became close friends. Shooting starts in El Toboso in mid-
April so perhaps you could be around. I shall try and come with
Yvonne [Cloetta] for the beginning and also the end when they
be will shooting in the Trappist Monastery of Oserre." (Tom
Burns is among the dedicatees of *Monsignor Quixote*.)

Tablet notice:
*The fortunes of Fr Quixote have been followed in the Christmas issues
of 1978 and 1980. Here is a third episode. Fr Quixote has taken a
holiday in his little car Rosinante with his friend Sancho, the
Communist ex-mayor of his village. Some of his misadventures have
come to the ears of his bishop, who is not amused. The novel in which
these episodes occur will be published next September by Bodley Head
under the title* Monsignor Quixote.

The door of Father Quixote's room opened and Father Herreira's voice announced, "His Excellency, the Bishop, is here."

Father Quixote had for a moment the odd impression that Father Herreira had suddenly grown old—the collar was the same blinding white, but the hair was white too and Father Herreira of course did not wear a bishop's ring or a big cross slung round his neck. But he would in time wear both, he certainly would in time, Father Quixote thought.

"I am sorry, Excellency. If you will give me a few minutes grace, I will be with you in the study."

"Stay where you are, Monsignor," the Bishop said. (He rolled out the title monsignor with an obvious bitterness.) He took from his sleeve a white silk handkerchief and dusted the chair beside the bed, looked carefully at the handkerchief to see how far it might have been soiled, lowered himself into the chair and put his hand on the sheet. But as Father Quixote was not in a position in which he could genuflect he thought it was permissible to leave out the kiss and the Bishop after a brief pause withdrew his hand. Then the Bishop pursed his lips and following a moment's reflection blew out the monosyllable: "Well!"

Father Herreira was standing in the doorway like a bodyguard. The Bishop told him, "You can leave me and the Monsignor—"the word seemed to burn his tongue for he made a grimace—"to have our little discussion alone." Father Herreira withdrew.

The Bishop clutched the cross on his purple *pechera* as though he were seeking a higher than human wisdom. It seemed like an anticlimax to Father Quixote when he said, "I trust you are feeling better."

"I am feeling perfectly well," Father Quixote replied. "My holiday has done me much good."

"Not if the reports I have received are true."

"What reports?"

"The Church always struggles to keep above politics."

"Always?"

"You know very well what I thought of your unfortunate involvement with the organisation *In Vinculis*."

"It was an impromptu act of charity, Excellency. I admit that I didn't really think ... Perhaps with charity one shouldn't think. Charity like love should be blind."

"You have been promoted for reasons quite beyond my comprehension to the rank of monsignor. A monsignor should always think. He must guard the dignity of the Church."

"I did not ask to be a monsignor. I do not like being a monsignor. The dignity of the parish priest of El Toboso is difficult enough to support."

"I do not pay attention to every rumour, Monsignor. The mere fact that a man is a member of Opus Dei does not necessarily make him a reliable witness. I will take your word if you give it to me that you didn't go into a certain shop in Madrid and ask to buy a cardinal's hat."

"That was not me. My friend made a harmless little joke ... "

"Harmless? That friend of yours, I believe, is a former mayor of El Toboso. A former Communist. You choose very unsuitable friends and travelling companions, Monsignor."

"I don't need to remind Your Excellency that our Lord ... "

"Oh yes, yes. I know what you are going to say. The text about publicans and sinners has always been very carelessly used to justify a lot of imprudence. St Matthew, chosen by our Lord, was a tax gatherer—a publican, a despised class. True enough, but there's a whole world of difference between a tax gatherer and a Communist."

"I suppose in some eastern countries it's possible to be both."

"I would remind *you*, Monsignor, that our Lord was the son of

God. To him all things were permissible, but for a poor priest like you or me isn't it more prudent to walk in the footsteps of St Paul? You know what he wrote to Titus—'There are many rebellious priests abroad, who talk of their own fantasies and lead men's minds astray: they must be silenced.'"

The Bishop paused to hear Father Quixote's response but none came. Perhaps he took this for a good sign, for when he spoke next, he dropped the monsignor and used the friendly and companionable "Father." "Your friend, Father," he said, "had apparently been drinking very heavily when you were both found. He didn't even wake when they spoke to him. Father Herreira noticed too that there was a great deal of wine in your car. I realise that in your nervous condition wine must have proved a serious temptation. Personally I always leave wine to the Mass. I prefer water. I like to pretend when I take a glass that I am drinking the pure water of Jordan."

"Perhaps not so pure," Father Quixote said.

"What do you mean, Father?"

"Well, Excellency, I can't help thinking of how Naaman, the Syrian, bathed seven times in the Jordan and left all his leprosy behind him in the water."

"An old Jewish legend from a very long time ago."

"Yes, I know that, Excellency, but still—after all it may be a true history—and leprosy is a mysterious disease. How many good Jewish people may follow the example of Naaman. Of course I agree with you that St Paul is a reliable guide and you will certainly remember that he also wrote to Titus—no, I am wrong, it was to Timothy: 'Do not confine thyself to water any longer; take a little wine to relieve thy stomach.'"

A period of silence descended on the bedroom. Father Quixote thought that perhaps the Bishop was seeking another quotation from St Paul, but he was wrong. The pause represented a change of subject rather than of mood. "What I don't understand, Monsignor, is that the Guardia found that you had exchanged clothes with this—this ex-mayor, this Communist."

"There was not an exchange of clothes, Excellency, only of a collar."

The Bishop closed his eyes. Impatience? Or he might have been praying for understanding.

"Why even a collar?"

"He thought I must be suffering from the heat in that kind of collar, so I gave it to him to try. I didn't want him to think I was claiming any special merit … A military uniform or even a Guardia's must be more difficult to endure in the heat than a collar. We are the lucky ones, Excellency."

"A story came to the ears of the parish priest in Valladolid that a bishop—or a monsignor—had been seen coming out of a scandalous film there—you know the kind of films which are shown now since the Generalissimo died …"

"Perhaps the poor monsignor did not know the kind of film he was attending. Sometimes titles are misleading."

"What was so shocking in the story is that—the bishop or the monsignor—you know how people can be confused by the *pechera* which you and I both wear—was seen coming out of this disreputable cinema laughing."

"Not laughing, Excellency, perhaps smiling."

"I don't understand your presence at such a film."

"I was deceived by the innocence of the title."

"Which was?"

"*A Maiden's Prayer.*"

The Bishop gave a deep sigh. "I sometimes wish," he said, "that the title of maiden were confined to Our Lady—and perhaps to members of religious orders. I realise you have been leading a very retired life in El Toboso, and you do not realise that the word 'maiden' used in our great cities in its merely temporary sense is often an incitement to lust."

"I admit, Excellency, that it had not occurred to me."

"Of course these are very minor matters in the eyes of the Guardia Civil, however scandalous they may appear in the eyes of the Church. But I and my colleague at Avila have had very great difficulty in persuading them to shut their eyes to what was a grave *criminal* offence. We had to approach a high authority in the Ministry of the Interior—luckily a member of Opus Dei ... "

"And a cousin I believe of Doctor Galván?"

"That is hardly relevant. He saw at once that it would do the Church untold harm if a monsignor appeared in the dock charged with helping a murderer to escape ... "

"Not a murderer, Excellency. He missed."

"A bank robber."

"No, no. It was a self-service store."

"I wish you wouldn't interrupt me with petty details. The Guardia in León found the man in possession of your shoes clearly marked inside with your name."

"It's a stupid habit of Teresa's. Poor thing, she means well, but she never trusts the cobbler to give the right pair back when he resoles them."

"I don't know whether it's deliberate, Monsignor, but you always seem to bring into our serious discussion quite trivial and irrelevant details."

"I am sorry—it wasn't my intention—I thought it might seem odd to you—my shoes being marked that way."

"What seems odd to me is your helping this criminal to escape the law."

"He did have a gun—but of course he would not have used it.

Shooting us would hardly have helped him."

"The Guardia in the end accepted that explanation, for the man had got rid of the gun and denied ever having had one. All the same they seem to have established that first you had hidden the man in the boot of your car and lied to a Guardia. You can't have done that under threat."

"I didn't lie, Excellency. Perhaps—well, I indulged in a little equivocation. The Guardia never directly asked whether he was in the boot. Of course I could plead a broad mental restriction! Father Herebert Jone points out that an accused criminal—I was legalistically speaking a criminal—may plead 'not guilty' which is only a conventional way of saying 'I am not guilty before law until I am proved guilty.' He even allows the criminal to say that the accusation is a calumny and may offer proofs for his pretended innocence—but there I think Father Herebert Jone goes a little too far."

"Who on earth is Father Herebert Jone?"

"A distinguished German moral theologian."

"I thank God that he's not a Spaniard."

"Father Herreira has a great respect for him."

"Anyway I haven't come here to talk about moral theology."

"I have always found it a very confusing subject, Excellency. For instance the concept of Natural Law ..."

"Nor have I come to talk about Natural Law. You have a remarkable talent, Monsignor, for straying from the real subject."

"Which is, Excellency?"

"The scandals you have been causing."

"But if I am accused of lies ... surely we are somewhere in the realm of moral theology."

"I am trying very very hard to believe," and the Bishop gave another prolonged sigh which made Father Quixote wonder with pity and not with satisfaction, whether the Bishop might possibly be suffering from asthma—"I repeat *very* hard, that you are too ill to realise what a dangerous situation you are in."

"Well, I suppose that applies to all of us."

"To all of us?"

"When we begin to think, I mean ..."

The Bishop gave a curious sound—it reminded Father Quixote of one of Teresa's hens laying an egg. "Ah," the Bishop said, "I was coming to that. Dangerous thought. Your Communist companion no doubt led you to think in ways ..."

"It wasn't that he *led* me, Excellency. He gave me the opportunity. You know in El Toboso—I'm very fond of the garagist (he looks so well after Rosinante), the butcher is a bit of a scoundrel—I don't mean that there's anything profoundly wrong in scoundrels, and of course there are the nuns who do make excellent liqueurs, but on this holiday I have felt a freedom ..."

"A very dangerous freedom it seems to have been."

"But he gave it to us didn't he—freedom? That was why they crucified him."

"Freedom," the Bishop said. It was like an explosion. "Freedom to break the law? You, a monsignor. Freedom to go to pornographic films? Help murderers?"

"No, no, I told you that he missed."

"And your companion—a Communist. Talking politics ..."

"No, no. We've discussed much more serious things than politics. Though I admit I hadn't realised that Marx had so nobly defended the Church."

"Marx?"

"A much misunderstood man, Excellency. I promise you."

"What books have you been reading on this—extraordinary—expedition?

"I always take with me St Francis de Sales. To please Father Herreira I took Father Herebert Jone with me too. And my friend lent me *The Communist Manifesto*—no, no, Excellency, it's not at all what you think it is. Of course I cannot agree with all his ideas, but there is a most moving tribute to religion—he speaks of 'the most heavenly ecstasies of religious fervour.'"

"I cannot sit here any longer and listen to the ravings of a sick mind," the Bishop said and rose.

"I have kept you here far too long, Excellency. It was a great act of charity on your part to come to see me in El Toboso. Doctor Galván will assure you that I am quite well."

"In the body perhaps. I think you need a different kind of doctor. I shall consult Dr Galván, of course, before I write to the Archbishop. And I shall pray."

"I am very grateful for your prayers," Father Quixote said. He noticed that the Bishop did not offer him his ring before leaving. Father Quixote reproached himself for having spoken too freely. "I have upset the poor man," he thought. Bishops, like the very poor and the uneducated, should be treated with a special prudence.

Whispers were to be heard from the passage outside his door. Then a key turned in the lock. So I am a prisoner, he thought, like Cervantes.

three

POETRY

17 October 1987

THE GRASS

Greene began his literary career with a book of verse, *Babbling April* (1925), which Harold Acton dismissed in the Oxford magazine *Cherwell* as "a diary of average adolescent moods". Greene later disowned the book. "The Grass", written in the mid-1980's, is a good example of a non-poet trying to develop a metaphor and producing a non-poem. (Grass-pushing-up-concrete is a platitude precisely because it has occurred to so many millions of intelligent people.) Nevertheless the poem is a curious slice of Greeniana.

> And the grass pushed its way
> with steadiness, silence,
> so many fractions, every thousand days,
> of a millimetre through the cement,
> and it doesn't matter how many pounds
> of walls and rooms; it went
> up through the doomed and yielding ground
> with the humility of violence.

And the blind love pushes its way,
like the grass through cement,
up through how many pounds of the past,
faces and failures and success,
so many fractions in a thousand days,
while the pressure of rooms grows less
and the mirrors twist and the old fireplaces
are shaken through the cement,
as the grass so certainly pushes its way,
and the love, towards what event?

four

REVIEWS

October 3rd, 1936
Fiction Chronicle

Stories of Three Decades. By Thomas Mann. Translated by H. T. Lowe-Porter. Secker & Warburg; pp. 567. 10s. 6d.
Steam Packet. By David Mathew. Longmans; pp. 148. 6s.

After the war, Thomas Mann was dismissed by younger German writers as a starchy man of letters; his fiction, with its lofty themes of nihilism, decadence and decay, seemed old-fashioned. However, Mann's status as a Teutonic Galsworthy was undermined in the mid-1970s when the embargo on his diaries expired. The diaries revealed that Mann was prone to bouts of nausea and homoerotic fantasies. Interestingly, Greene thought the homosexual hero (Herr Aschenbach) of Mann's celebrated novella *Death in Venice* was a "self-portrait", but his perceptiveness was unusual at the time. In 1936 when Greene reviewed Mann for *The Tablet*, the German writer was the perfect paterfamilias who had fathered six children; he radiated a stolid mercantile air, indeed, and was upheld as a virtuous anti-Nazi émigré after Goebbels banned all mention of his name from German newspapers. Father (later Archbishop) David Mathew was godfather to Greene's daughter Lucy Caroline. (His brother Gervase, a Dominican priest, was the dedicatee of *The Power and the Glory*.) In 1963, Archbishop Mathew was made resident priest at Stonor, one of the Catholic houses which had sheltered Edmund Campion before his arrest by Queen Elizabeth I's police. Mathew had written biographies of James I, Lady Jane Gray and Charles I, as well as novels.

Not since the death of Henry James has a novelist occupied so solitary a position in the world of letters as Herr Thomas Mann. It is peculiarly and ironically right for an author who has devoted almost his whole career to a study of the solitary, the isolated, the exiled, to be not only himself a type of the solitary artist, but also an exile from his country, from the simple regimented human hoard for whom he has always expressed the unreciprocated love of the man on the outside looking in.

Always: for the most astonishing characteristic of Herr Mann's genius has been its early maturity. It is not rare for a poet to produce his finest work by the age of twenty-five, but for a novelist to complete a prose work so full, so serene, with such an undercurrent of poetry and philosophy, as *Buddenbrooks* by that age is astonishing. Young men more usually write from their nerves than from their intellect: tumultuously and with untidy passion.

Astonishment is increased by this collection in one volume of Herr Mann's shorter tales. More than half of these were written before he was thirty; at twenty he wrote *Little Herr Friedemann*, his first study of the isolated spirit, a story with hardly a trace of immaturity or of undisciplined talent, except possibly in the abruptness of the close, and at twenty-six he had written *Tonio Kröger* which he himself classes with his major works, with *Death in Venice* and *The Magic Mountain*. *Tonio Kröger* is his first explicit study of what he believes to be the creative disease, and the method in most of his stories (the sharp glitter, the almost chromium lines of *The Blood of the*

Walsungs is an exception), is as far removed as possible from that of James, who also concerned himself to an unusual extent with the creative temperament. James' main technical interest was in dramatisation; "dramatise, dramatise", the voice used to whisper in his ear at Grosvenor House dinners, but Herr Mann as early as *Tonio Kröger*, and as late as *The Young Joseph*, quite magnificently disregards what is usually considered the novelist's first duty. His characters are always—physically—vivid (when they are writers, like Herr Spinell in *Tristan*, they are usually a little grotesque), but when they open their mouths, the same God speaks, with the same subdued poetic passion.

What gives importance to Herr Mann's treatment of isolation (probably only an intimate knowledge of pre-war Germany, of all that led up to the war and the Third Reich, would explain the overwhelming personal passion Herr Mann puts into that theme) is that the artist's problem is not unique, it is shared by the drunkard in *The Way to the Churchyard*, by the hunchback in *Little Herr Friedemann*, by the Jew and his beloved twin sister in *The Blood of the Walsungs*. Herr Mann has expressed with greater passion and insight than any other writer the peculiar nostalgia of our time and our class: "a longing for the innocent, the simple, and the living, for a little friendship, devotion, familiar human happiness—the gnawing, surreptitious hankering for the bliss of the commonplace." The isolation of the artist, his genius regarded as a disease ("What they"—the simple and living—"cannot comprehend is that a properly constituted healthy decent man never writes, acts or composes"). These themes in *Tonio Kröger* are treated more or less on the level of calm debate, but increasingly, perhaps as Herr Mann feels the isolation with more personal bitterness, the note of self-hatred creeps into his work, the diseased man blaming his weakness, the writer loathing his own genius. Tonio is not a figure of fun, as Herr Spinell, the suffering, affected, cowardly little novelist at Davos, is, and passages in *Death in Venice* are like a blow struck in the author's own face (the date was 1911, war was threatening Europe, the unhappy isolation of the man who could not go with the happy and simple crowd had never previously in Germany been so acute). The presentation of Herr Aschenbach, the distinguished, the classical novelist, who had won fame "almost before he was out of high school," reads, in some of its details, like a deliberate self-portrait, and the fantasy which follows has some of the horror of a self-inflicted wound: the dumb, frightened, pagan infatuation which leads to the dyed hair and the cosmetics in the little Italian barber's shop.

> "There he sat, the master: this was he who had found a way to reconcile art and honours; who had written *The Abject*, and in a style of classic purity renounced bohemianism and all its works, all sympathy with the abyss and the troubled depths of the outcast human soul. This was he who had put knowledge underfoot to climb so high; who had outgrown the ironic pose and adjusted himself to the burdens and obligations of fame; whose renown had been officially recognised and his name ennobled, whose style was set for a model in the schools. There he sat. His eyelids were closed, there was only a swift, sidelong glint of the eyeballs now and again, something between a question and a leer; while the rouged and flabby mouth uttered single words of the sentences shaped in his disordered brain by the fantastic logic that governs our dreams."

The words he speaks are from Plato. This is the real, the overpowering, ennui of paganism. Is it possible, one exclaims, for a man so to hate the genius which gives his career significance? Mann's sense of evil is as strong as James' but James set the moral struggle in a Christian setting, he hovered, regretfully and with a sense of enormous daring, on the edge of the Catholic Church, while to Mann, whose style is coloured by Greece, evil is more than anything else the mere absence of peace, happiness, the health of which he feels that his genius, that "disease", has defrauded him.

Dr. David Mathew's *Steam Packet* is the experiment of an historian who is also a poet. Very conscious, very selective, with a sense of hidden malice and subdued poetry, it describes the company on board the Calais-Dover steam packet on a late April day in 1838: a company more than usually varied, for foreign envoys are crossing the Channel, each with his personal servants, to the Coronation. The exact period detail is beautifully and unobtrusively worked in, even to the iron shelter and the metal footwarmer on Calais pier, nor do the characters themselves in their thoughts and their careful cramped judicious actions ever falsify their period. I feel that the author may have been most at home with the young Count of Lombay, a disappointed Royalist, a Catholic a little suspicious of the dignitaries of his own Church, with the kind of melancholy, fastidious mind which carries indelibly the print of many alien atmospheres. "He thought of the *Cristinos* and their financiers and the trail of sordid unavowable transaction. It seemed to him that there was about the due order of the great palaces some ultimate delicacy of perception based on austerity. A sense of honour must ultimately be austere and there was the Escorial and, a bare six years ago, the Court of Charles X in exile at Holyrood, the *Maison de France* with its shadowy ceremony, very dignified and tired in the Scottish rain." This to my mind is the most remarkable achievement of a book which excites admiration on every page: that though the author is so intimately at home with the Lombay mind, he can present, say, Mr. Burnaby, the British engineer, ponderous and progressive, or Mr. Harker, the major-domo of the Austrian Ambassador, astute, corruptible, with a friendly taste for liquor, from the same exactly measured distance, without a trace of over-emphasis, of caricature at a cruder level. As to the effect of the style I cannot do better than quote the Count of Lombay, as he picks at Balzac: "How just, how damaging this train of adjectives, and a thin definite satisfaction rose to the surface of his mind as he took up the paper knife to separate the pages just ahead," but that does less than justice to the curious edge of poetry which surrounds this shipload as closely as the Channel fog, which secures them from life for art.

October 24th, 1936
Fiction Chronicle

Midnight. By Julien Green[1]. Translated by Vyvian Holland.
Heinemann. 7s. 6d.
Novel on Yellow Paper. By Stevie Smith. Cape. 7s. 6d.
And Then You Wish. By John van Druten. Michael Joseph. 8s. 6d.
The Splendour Falls. By Romilly Cavan. Dent. 7s. 6d.

Julien Green, born in Paris of American parents, was a
troubled Catholic novelist "crucified", as he put it, "in sex".
In his review of *Midnight* (the novel was translated by Oscar
Wilde's son Vyvian Holland), Greene announces: "I do not
know if M. Green is a Catholic", yet Monsieur Green was
then living in London off the Brompton Road and hard at
work on his Catholic novel *Le Malfaiteur* (published as *The
Transgressor*). Greene surely knew that his near namesake
was a Catholic? In 1936 Stevie Smith was not yet known as a
poet. *Novel on Yellow Paper*, completed in just ten weeks and
originally entitled *Pompey Camilus*, is a gossipy stream-of-
consciousness soliloquy indebted to Virginia Woolf. (One
reader, assuming the author's name to be pseudonymous,
actually wrote to Woolf: "You are Stevie Smith. No doubt of
it. And *Yellow Paper* is far and away your best book".) Oddly,
Greene detects in Smith a "dislike" of the Catholic
theologian Ronald Knox, yet Smith hugely admired him.
(Evelyn Waugh, incidentally, was later to write Knox's
biography.) John van Druten, no longer fashionable, was
once Britain's most successful playwright. His celebrated
play, *I Am a Camera* (1951), adapted Sally Bowles' story from
Christopher Isherwood's *Goodbye to Berlin*, and was later
turned into the 1972 film *Cabaret*. Romilly Cavan is now
quite forgotten (but clearly she was not worth reading in
1936).

Reviewers are sometimes accused of not reading the books they notice. I have read every page of all these books, with one exception. Miss Cavan's defeated me on the seventy-third page. Nevertheless "tasting" is more legitimate than it sounds, and the first paragraph of most books tells you what to expect. Is not the whole impudence of *Tristram Shandy* in this: "I wish either my father or my mother, or indeed both of them, as they were in duty both equally bound to it, had minded what they were about when they begot me"; the grim Puritanism of *The Scarlet Letter* in this: "A throng of bearded men, in sad-coloured garments, and grey, steeple-crowned hats, intermixed with women, some wearing hoods, and others bareheaded, was assembled in front of a wooden edifice, the door of which was heavily timbered with oak, and studded with iron spikes"; the intense moral passion of *The Wings of the Dove* in: "She waited, Kate Croy, for her father to come in, but he kept her unconscionably, and there were moments at which she showed herself, in the glass over the mantel, a face positively pale with the irritation that had brought her to the point of going away without sight of him"? An artist is unlikely to show his purpose with more conviction and concentration than in the moment when he first sets pen to paper.

Let me quote, not in any order, the first sentences of these books, and see how they compare with those great beginnings. I think it will be agreed that only one comes off with any credit.

A. "It took very little to make Blanche happy, so little that Muriel Stapleton had once compared her to the White Queen: 'A little kindness and putting her hair in papers would do wonders with her.' And as she left the flat where she had been having tea with Muriel's mother, Blanche was very happy, with a warm, bright day-dream happiness, more appropriate to eighteen than fifty-eight, that went with her all the way back to West Hampstead, suffusing her in the 'bus with a mild, sweet benignity like spilled ointment."

B. "Towards the end of a winter day, beneath a grey sky swept by an icy wind, a carriage was slowly rolling its way along a track bordered by ploughed fields. It was the sort of conveyance which is never seen anywhere nowadays, save in the provinces, a sort of black box perched above wheels that were far too big for it, with cloth blinds covering the windows, and two big metal lamps to right and left of the coachman."

C. "Beginning this book (not as they say 'book' in our trade—they mean magazine), beginning this book, I should like if I may, I should like, if I may (that is the way Sir Phoebus writes), I should like them to say: 'Goodbye to all my friends, my beautiful and lovely friends.'"

D. "Barrier, the overgrown, meandering village, was smugly beautiful in late afternoon calm. The morrow of Good Friday seemed to throw some mystic aura of beatitude upon it, making it less than its usual self in bright spring guise, yet no less certain of its careful charm in being of the sea and yet not with it."

I don't think a reviewer would be unfair if he decided that only B (M. Julian Green's *Midnight*) was worth serious attention, though he might expect to get fun of a kind from C (Miss Stevie Smith's *Novel on Yellow Paper*).

To begin with A, this is from Mr. van Druten's gentle, ambling and expensive tale, which many elderly and lonely middle-class ladies with artistic interests may enjoy. It is the story of just such a lady who takes possessive control of a young playwright. His plays have never yet been produced, and he works in an office. Somehow, by sheer insistence she makes a dramatic critic, whom she finds in the next seat at an experimental theatre, read his latest effort, and then the course we have foreseen for a long while is clear: success and the young man's abandonment of tiresome, possessive and pathetic Blanche. The story is a much too long, commonplace essay in easy pathos, neither well nor very badly written. Mr. Ford Madox Ford, in his admirable book on the English novel, divided fiction into novels and nuvvels.[2] This is a "nuvvel".

If you read fiction with half a mind and prefer a pale reflection of familiar life, soothing and superficial, this is your book. The opening sentence tells you that and more: the loose thoughtless method by which the author drifts from one mind to another, neither fully accepting the advantages of an omniscient observer, nor the unity which confinement to a single mind would have given him: a sloppy technique. Mr. van Druten is a dramatist, but he never dramatises here; like the old stage butler, he prefers to tell you all about his characters rather than allow them to express themselves in speech and gait and action. A dramatist should know better than to write like this: "Her panic flooded away and left behind it nothing but emptiness, a void, an echoing hollow which was her life from now on." All Mr. van Druten's words mean less than they say, like the words in a leading article; they are the opposite of true poetic writing where words are used concretely as symbols, with layers of poetic meaning.

B is an example of poetic writing. No voids and echoing hollows here. The wintry scene, the old cab and the cloth blinds, all M. Green's images are objective, and like the "black box" which immediately puts us in mind of a coffin, they awake implications. The whole story, of the child orphaned by her mother's suicide, who escapes from one guardian to another until she reaches the strange household of poor relations, sheltering from the world under the rule of the mystic, M. Edmé, and chooses disastrously, against her real desire, the stupid handsome lover, instead of the life of the spirit, is prepared in that opening paragraph. M. Green is sometimes treated by critics as a mere fantasist, a peculiarly inaccurate criticism to bring against an author with so vivid a sense of this world (the distant train with a noise "like the hurried limping of some giant insect"; the woman babbling of her dead children as she casts her eyes around the drawingroom: "she looked as though she were wandering about in a cemetery, looking for a grave whose exact position she had forgotten"; the fat woman suffocating under her weight of flesh who "had the look of someone sunk in a quicksand until only her eyes remained"). M. Green's world only seems fantastic to critics who have retained no religious sense. The world in his pages has always the dark clarity of woodlands silhouetted against an advancing storm; he can describe an umbrella drying before the fire, so that it becomes the image of a whole human character; like a man condemned to death his memories are exact and nostalgic. The little stuffy French provincial rooms open on eternity as the clock strikes. It is Mr. van Druten's characters who are dreamlike and half-realised. As Mr. Eliot has said: "With the disappearance of the idea of Original Sin, with the disappearance of the idea of intense moral struggle, the human beings presented to us both in poetry and in prose fiction today, tend to become less and less real." I do not know if M. Green is a Catholic: he is certainly a religious writer of the highest talent, whose novels should be particularly acceptable to Catholic readers.

Both Miss Smith (C) and Miss Cavan (D) have tried their best to avoid writing "nuvvels". Miss Smith's novel (her publishers compare it with Sterne's) is blessedly fresh in form—a long slangy interior monologue wandering back and forth in time—and often shrewd and amusing in content. (She has a particular dislike for Father Martindale and Father Knox, but surely her admirably winged remarks on "hearty" Christianity apply more to the Anglican than the Catholic Church?).

November 14th, 1936
Fiction Chronicle

Nightwood. By Djuna Barnes. Faber and Faber. 10s.6d.
Of Mortal Love. By William Gerhardi[3]. Arthur Barker. 8s. 6d.
Antigua, Penny, Puce. By Robert Graves. Constable. 7s. 6d.
The Missing Miniature. By Erich Kästner. Translated by C.H. Brooks.
  Cape. 7s. 6d.
Parody Party. Hutchinson. 8s. 6d.

T .S. Eliot was known to keep a photograph of Djuna Barnes in his office next to one of Groucho Marx. (She "looks nice", agreed Ernest Hemingway.) The American-born Barnes had made a splash in 1936 with her fictional fantasia *Nightwood* (original title: *Anatomy of Night*), which Dylan Thomas considered one of the "three best novels by women". Reportedly Barnes wrote it after the ending of her tumultuous affair with the lesbian artist Thelma Wood. Greene, like Eliot, admired the Jacobean richness of the novel's prose. William Gerhardie published his first novel, *Futility*, in 1922 after touting it round thirteen British publishers. However, his essentially autobiographical talent had apparently become exhausted by 1936; *Of Mortal Love* wins scant praise from Greene. Robert Graves' poisonous novel of English manners, *Antigua, Penny, Puce*, was adored by most critics at the time, including Greene. ("Only four unfavourable notices of my A.P.P., out of more than 100, have hitherto appeared in England", Graves wrote to a hapless newspaper editor in 1936. "This includes the one in your Jan 15 issue. By a queer fatality the publication of the first two – in *News Chronicle*, *Observer* – was in each case followed by the sudden death of the reviewer.") Graves' novel was later much admired by the dyspeptic Philip Larkin. Erich Kästner, author of *Emil and the Detectives* (1929), was one of the outstanding children's writers of the 20th century; Greene recommends his work to any level of brow and age. *Parody Party*, a collection of literary spoofs, was a Christmas tie-in with contributions from John Betjeman, Cyril Connolly, Rose Macaulay and Rebecca West. Douglas Woodruff's contribution, 'The English Week-End', parodies Dean Inge of St. Paul's and his Anglican distaste for Rome. ("I do not suggest that no Roman Catholics wash. There are exceptions.") Greene was more impressed by Connolly's parody of Aldous Huxley, which features a drug-peddling butler ("Snuff, peotl buds, hashish or Indian hemp, sir?"). Greene agreed with Connolly that Huxley had lost much of his mordant brilliance in his drug-befuddled Los Angeles exile. Greene himself loved literary pastiche; under a false name he came second place in a *New Statesman* competition in 1949 for a parody of his own style.

More than twelve years ago Miss Djuna Barnes published a short story called *Aller et Retour* in Mr. Ford Madox Ford's brilliant and short-lived *Transatlantic Review*. It was an impressive story with a cruel, visual wit and dialogue curiously precise and suggestive, like the imagery of a Jacobean dramatist. Madam Bartmann, a middle-aged and rather absurd Madame Bovary, who returned to see her child after her husband had died (a rather unnecessary journey it turned out to be, for the child was safely engaged to a sedate clerk in Government employ) spoke like a character in one of Webster's plays: "Horses hurry you away from danger, trains bring you back to the scene of your corruption." *Nightwood*, Miss Barnes' first novel, is from the same mould; twelve years have only increased the layers of suggestion; the shady Catholic doctor, O'Connor, has taken the place of Madame Bartmann as the mouthpiece, the commentator, and his message is much the same. "A murderer," Madame Bartmann said, "has less prejudice than a saint. Sometimes it is better to be a saint. Do not be vain about your indifference, should you be possessed of indifference; and don't misconceive the value of your voluptuousness; it is only seasoning to the whole horror."

"The whole horror"—it is from a horror of life that Miss Barnes' work springs, and her book, it is to be carefully noted, is no more for general and indiscriminate reading than is Mr. Joyce's *Ulysses*. It is sometimes obscene, though never pornographic: "gaudy, cheap cuts from the beast life," and it leaves the impression that the author herself might not inaptly be described in terms used of a character: "a religious woman without the joy and safety of the Catholic faith, which at a pinch covers up the spots on the wall when the family portraits take a slide." The whole book is an exaggerated reaction against the world by someone who has been bitten by faith, but faith gone wild and dangerous with despair. The dramatic bones of the story, the love of Nora Flood for Robin Vote, a woman driven to excess by an uprooted hopelessness, whose end is as horrible as anything conceived by Webster or Tourneur, is the least satisfactory part of the book: there are times when the hidden emotion is too strong for the phrases used and the result is a little absurd: Robin herself is insufficiently objectified. What makes the book remarkable is partly the conciseness of the incidental portraits, the way in which Miss Barnes defines a character ("She had a continual rapacity for other people's facts; absorbing time, she held herself responsible for historic characters. She was avid and disorderly in her heart. She defiled the very meaning of personality in her passion to be a person. Somewhere about her was the tension of the accident that made the beast the human endeavour"), when each sentence is like a marking shot which leads to the conclusive bull, but mainly the rhetoric of Dr. O'Connor, who reveals the individual disaster against the huge spiritual skyscape. "In time everything is possible and in space everything forgivable; life is but the intermediary vice. There is eternity to blush in." And again: "I've done, and been, everything that I didn't want to be or do—Lord, put the light out—so I stand here, beaten up and mauled and weeping, knowing I am not what I thought I was, a good man doing wrong, but the wrong man doing nothing much … I talk too much because I have been made so miserable by what you are keeping hushed." A sick spiritual condition may have gone to this book, but it is rare in contemporary fiction to be able to trace any spiritual experience whatever, and the accent, I think, is sometimes that of a major poet.

An enormous gap, as deep as it is wide, separates Miss Barnes' novel from Mr. Gerhardi's. Dinah Fry, pretty, unsophisticated, with a kind of agile pathos, was first married to Jim. Then she lived with Walter and was divorced by Jim. Then she left Walter and lived with Beano. Then Beano left her, and she tried to make up her mind whether she would return to Walter or marry Eric. Then she died of diphtheria. It would be unfair to emphasise too much this difference of worlds, between "So I, doctor Mattew Mighty O'Connor, ask you to think of the night the day long, and of the day the night through, or at some reprieve of the brain it will come upon you heavily—an engine stalling itself upon your chest, halting its wheels against your heart; unless you have made a roadway for it," and "If there were no marriages the child would live with the more congenial parent. All the legislation necessary in the case of people living together is that in the event of their having a child one third of the joint income …" and so on, for Mr. Gerhardi is not trying to write a novel with spiritual implications—or is he? There are moments when he looks rather wistfully, like a girl through the window of a fashionable dressmaker's, towards eternity, life after death, the spirit, things he cannot afford if he is to retain those agreeable traits of blitheness, light pathos, an amorality which would be more charming if it were a little less elegant and practised: there are times when Mr. Gerhardi writes like a professional seducer. He deals with much the same society as Mr. Evelyn Waugh but with a pouting tenderness, not with satire. The author of *Futility* and *The Polyglots* has great talent, but he never quite achieves anything completely memorable. The last scenes in the fever hospital when Walter, Eric and Beano wait for the tiresome, possessive and attractive Dinah to die, while the rain showers fitfully down into the little yard with its single elm and its wooden fence, beyond the swing doors and the central heating pipes, is finely and exactly imagined. It is a magnificent and moving finale for something not quite worth it.

One can give a Universal Certificate (to borrow a term from the British Board of Film Censors) to the other books on this list. *Antigua, Penny, Puce* is the most amusing novel I have read for many months: a rare postage stamp is the excuse for a quarrel between a brother and a sister and for intrigues which attain Machiavellian subtlety. Like most good comedies the book deals with characters who would be quite unbearable in life, and their unbearability is the occasion for a series of wildly funny situations, inside and outside the Law Courts. A very original novel with a humour which reminded me, in its heartlessness and its irresponsibility, of a Marx Brothers' film.

The Missing Miniature is by the author of *Fabian* and *Emil and the Detectives*. The political situation in Germany is, one imagines, responsible for the development of the author from *Emil* rather than from *Fabian*, from the lightest and most amusing fantasy rather than from his nervous and bitter social satire. Herr Kästner's new novel is an *Emil* for adults, quick, good-humoured, fantastic nonsense, as puffy and pleasant as a German creamy cake, about a crime of Wodehousian complexity and criminals of superb resource. It is a novel one can confidently recommend.

Parody Party is not another *Christmas Garland*[4], but then Mr. Max Beerbohm had writers of more importance to parody, and his exact and tender treatment would have been tedious if directed against the

more popular writers represented here. The symposium has some
excellent contributions: I particularly enjoyed Mr. Douglas
Woodruff's *Dean Inge* and Mr. Cyril Connolly's *Aldous Huxley*, a
Huxley already gone a little "gamey" and on the verge of discovering
pacifism and a personal religion. I feel that Miss Rebecca West's
Sepulchre: a Tale of Mors, Seventh Viscount and Twelfth Baron Sepulchre
misses the style of her subject: the faded George Moore monotonies,
the sudden incursions, during emotional moments, of the Authorised
Version. Mr. Francis Iles' *Close Season in Polchester* is nearer the mark,
in spite of a crude beginning. He has everything here: the loose,
unbuttoned style, the conscious connoisseurship, the violent
melodrama, and the sadistic incidents of Mr. Walpole's fiction.

Geoffrey Wylde sketching the thirty-three-year-old Graham Greene for the *London Mercury* in 1937, shortly before the writer's departure for Mexico.

January 9th, 1937
Fiction Chronicle

Salavin. By Georges Duhamel. Translated by G. Billings. Dent. 8s. 6d.
The Big Money. By John Dos Passos. Constable. 7s. 6d.
The Law and the McLaughlins. By Margaret Wilson. Cassell. 7s. 6d.

Georges Duhamel was known chiefly for his two long novel-cycles, *Salavin* and *The Pasquier Chronicles*, which were intended to form a "humane and subtle" criticism of Christianity. Greene, however, found the French author's talent too "delicate and sentimental"; Duhamel's passionate attack on Nazi despotism, *The Darkness of the Third Reich*, published in 1939, might have been more to his liking. The *Big Money* was the third volume of Dos Passos' electrifying epic of high-pressure life in America, *U.S.A.* To mark its publication, *Time Magazine* had put Dos Passos on its front cover and hailed *The Big Money* as modern Dickens, but Greene was not impressed and thought the characters lacked depth. *The Big Money* nevertheless provides an exceptionally powerful commentary on the wealth and corruption of contemporary America, and why Greene should have thought that Margaret Wilson wrote better novels than Dos Passos is a mystery. (Wilson was known for her fiction set in British India; unlike Dos Passos, she is no longer read.)

Salavin is a long, and for the most part intensely subjective, novel about a man possessing no religious faith, who yet formed the resolution to become a saint. A small clerk in a Paris office, he was dismissed because he gave way to a sudden absurd impulse to touch his employer's ear with his finger, and the first of the four short novels which are bound up here in one volume describes the privations he then suffered. This novel is in the form of a monologue addressed to a stranger in a bar, and it was published seven years before the succeeding volume, which consists of *Salavin's Journal.*

This long book has been, I think, rather excessively praised. It is a scrappy work. One has no conviction that M. Duhamel foresaw in the first volume the course his novel was to take. He was content there to draw a picture of a lonely, introspective man. He does this admirably with a charming minor poetic feeling for places as well as people. "If you go through the Rue Lhomond late in the evening, at the hour when the noises of Paris are lulling themselves to sleep, you will hear under your feet the sound of all the sewers of Mont Ste. Geneviève droning softly as though they were far distant waterfalls. Those are my waterfalls, the waterfalls of my journeys." And again: "Your house, the place where you live," Salavin says, "becomes an image of yourself after a while. It's the only thing you know and you see it mirrored in all its sadness—unbelievable sadness." He generalizes on his unfortunate encounter with his employer: "There was a man, just an ordinary man like you or me, and yet such a barrier existed between us that I couldn't even touch a part of him with the tip of my finger without becoming a culprit. Then I'm not really free? I'm surrounded, am I, as maritime countries are, by waters that are inviolate, in which strangers can't navigate without permission?" His only human contact is his mother. "She had to call me several times before I came up to the surface of the world again. I've always thought that my mother knew instinctively about this desertion of my spirit, and her summons was rather like the cry of an animal when her little ones are in danger." These quotations may give an idea of the charm, sentiment and minor poetry of the first novel.

It is a pity that M. Duhamel after seven years went back to this character. He wanted, for his purposes, a clerk who had consistently failed at any large success, and I suppose he remembered the timid Salavin and thought that by using him again he would escape what is a novelist's most difficult, but surely his most interesting task, that of giving some idea of the "dark backward and abysm" of time. Unfortunately *this* dark backward doesn't fit. It is quite a new Salavin we meet in the journal. He has been married for nearly ten years, for many years he has been the trusted employee of the Pasteurised and Oxygenated Milk Company. The old Salavin was not interested in the question of success, which haunts the later Salavin until he decides that since fame in science, art, politics, war or finance is denied him, he will become a saint. This is a very methodical Salavin who gives himself fifteen years, who daily notes his success or failure, and lest his wife should read his journal substitutes the word "tourist" for saint. *Salavin's Journal* is the most interesting of the four novels: it shows how an irreligious man bent on sanctity (which he defines as "humane conduct") is driven to adopt the technique, if I may use the term, of the traditional saint. The body, he soon discovers, must be mortified if the mind is to remain alert ("Fortune comes now and then to the man who sleeps but not saintliness"), family ties weaken him so that he has to leave his wife, and finally we watch him nibbling uneasily round faith itself. There is an admirably satiric portrait of a fashionable Protestant "saint" who combines psycho-analysis with the confessional. Salavin writes to him: "Dear Pastor Croquet: a lost unhappy soul seeks your help …" and receives in answer two typewritten lines: "Pastor Croquet will receive M. Louis Salavin the 29th November at 9.30." In the upper left hand corner of the paper are the initials: C.A.F.A. At the bottom of the page: "S, 948. For future correspondence refer to this number." At last Salavin, by his practise of chastity and his self-mortification and his good works, reaches the point of writing: "I want an immortal soul or else nothing at all."

The two books which follow the Journal seem to me the weakest. *The Lyonnais Club*, where Salavin is seen involved innocently in a revolutionary circle, and the final novel, *End of Illusion*, in which he leaves France for Morocco, practises charity on a heroic scale in a native hospital, and dies, rather sentimentally, in his wife's arms, of a gangrened leg, add nothing to what should have been the climax: "I want an immortal soul." M. Duhamel in these two books has tried to draw Salavin from the outside, but his talent is mainly subjective. There is nothing in common between the Salavin of the confession and the Salavin of the Journal, and there is not much more in common between the Salavin of the Journal and the objective Salavin of the Moroccan hospital, a bitter suspicious, rather Gauguinesque figure. Those who trumpet *Salavin* into the immortal list do a disservice to M. Duhamel, whose delicate and slightly sentimental talent has so happily flowered in the Pasquier chronicles.

There was a time … so one begins regretfully to write about Mr. Dos Passos, but was there ever really a time when this novelist, whose originality has been confined to the rather superficial inventions of the Camera Eye and the News Reel, and the interpolation into his narrative of brief biographies of real people, promised to be anything more than a worthy heavy-handed Socialist Galsworthy. In his painstaking panorama of the post-war years, the biographies (this time of Ford, Insull, Isadora Duncan) are far more vivid than the characters. Mr. Dos Passos' theme, the moral degradation and the brutality which accompany capitalism, is worthy of respect, but no good fairy endowed him with the gift of narrative or of characterization. "Mary French had never worked so hard in her life. She wrote releases, got up statistics on T.B., undernourishment of children, sanitary conditions, crime, took trips on inter-urban trollies and slow locals to Rankin and Braddock … " so the novel drones on: sympathy founded on statistics. Compare it with this passage from Miss Margaret Wilson's novel, in which a human passion does seem to speak: "Tragedy doesn't elevate and purify people's feelings … 'Out, out, damned spot' they write. And poetry makes you forget the real thing. The real thing is that a cruel woman made her husband kill a poor old good man. And they write, 'Out, out, damned spot,' so that the words sing like a song in your ears. Remorse isn't anything poetic. I guess I know! And now all the town talks of the murderers. They go walking on Sundays past the jail, to look at the place where they are, even if they can't see them. And who thinks of that woman who is left a widow? What's she doing today? Nobody knows. Nobody cares … They forget the real fact because the trial is so interesting."

The real fact—that is what Miss Wilson, unlike Mr. Dos Passos, never forgets. She has an admirable gift for very simple direct narrative, and her theme has always been passionately realized in terms of human beings. Her previous novel, *The Valiant Wife*, is to me the most memorable historical novel of the last three years. *The Law and the McLaughlins* is less satisfactory, for unless this is part of a much longer work, she has allowed the real subject to slip out of the centre of her picture: the life of a woman who loves and marries an escaped lyncher and lives under the constant fear of discovery, who devotes herself, cold-bloodedly as it were, to good works, so that when the hour she dreads strikes, she may have friends in the town to help her husband. It is astonishing to me that Miss Wilson, unless she purposes to return to it, should allow this subject to be pushed into the background. Nevertheless, unsatisfying though this novel is compared with *The Valiant Wife* or *The Dark Duty*, we are always aware of a writer of fine moral discrimination and a passionate awareness of individual suffering.

January 30th, 1937

Fiction Chronicle

Bread and Wine. By Ignazio Silone. Translated by Gwenda David and
Eric Mosbacher. Methuen. 7s. 6d.
Pie in the Sky. By Arthur Calder-Marshall. Cape. 8s. 6d.
Eggs and Baker. By John Masefield. Heinemann. 7s. 6d.

Ignazio Silone, sometime Communist, later anti-Communist
and alleged Fascist informer, first came to Greene's attention
in 1934 when he praised his novel *Fontamara* (in *The Spectator*)
as a "moving account of Fascist brutality". Alone among Anglo
Catholic critics, Greene noted the dense scriptural symbolism
and bitter humour of the author's sequel novel, *Bread and Wine.*
("Critics who see me only as some kind of sociological or
political writer", Silone wrote, "have never been to my
liking".) Arthur Calder-Marshall had made his name in 1933
with publication of his novel *Two of a Kind*, which was said to
contain a hidden obscenity ("they came, together"). A
contemporary of Greene's at Oxford, in later years Calder-
Marshall exchanged quite caustic letters with his friend. ("I
don't know whether Bruce Marshall is in Antibes", Greene
wrote to Arthur in 1967, "and even though he is your cousin I
won't go out of my way to discover! I hate his books".) John
Masefield, the Poet Laureate, was an immensely popular
writer in pre-war Britain, whose *Collected Poems* (1923) had sold
over 80,000 copies. For the most part his readers were middle-
brow conservatives as reluctant to take a stand on literature as
they were on the events unfolding in pre-war Spain and
Germany. Yet *Egg and Baker* (subtitled "The Days of Trial"),
contains an unforgettable portrait of a heartless landowner in
1870s England, and in fact is a politically engaged novel in the
Silonian mould. Masefield, the establishment poet with links
to royalty, was apparently at heart a socialist, and that is partly
why Greene admired the novel.

Bread and Wine is about Fascism and the Church in Italy. It is a bitter, humane and humorous book with an honesty and thoughtfulness which raises it right out of the rank of political and propagandist novels. The author is an enemy of the Church as he sees it today, but one might say of him as he writes of one of his characters: "His voice was not that of an atheist but that of a disappointed lover." An enemy of Signor Silone's quality (there is real spiritual beauty in a mind capable of drawing the character of Spina and Don Benedetto) deserves the respectful attention of all Catholics. His criticism is not hasty, shallow or partisan, and if the Church is to avoid in Italy the cruel and undiscriminating retribution she has suffered in Spain, she must show herself capable of winning back the loyalty of men like Signor Silone.

For this story of Spina, a conspirator against the Totalitarian State who re-enters Italy and works among the peasants, disguised as a priest, is not of the usual Left-Wing type, blindly self-righteous. "He had broken with the old world and all its comforts, cut himself off from his family, abandoned his favourite studies, set himself to live for justice and truth alone, and entered a party in which he was told that justice and truth were petty-bourgeois prejudices. Did he not feel himself betrayed?" The motive behind his Socialism is profoundly Christian, and the theme of the book is less noble Socialism pitted against ignoble Fascism (the stock-in-trade of every Left-Wing novelist) than the plight of a Catholic in a society which seems to him to deny most of the qualities he recognizes in Christianity. "They made me learn the catechism by heart when I was a boy. The catechism says: 'to give drink to the thirsty, to clothe the naked, to give shelter to pilgrims and to succour the sick.' The catechism does not say: 'to succour the sick who are of the same way of thinking as you.' All the catechism says is to succour the sick. But in those days the Church was for the People and not for the

Government. But perhaps they have changed the catechism now, too."

. The poetic quality in this novel, rare in political fiction, comes, I think, from the angle of writing. *Bread and Wine* opens with a small party given by an old priest, Don Benedetto, in his country retirement, to his former pupils. Don Benedetto is not a politician, he doesn't work against the Totalitarian State ("It is not as an elector but as a man that I find this society intolerable"), but as another character remarks, "In the Land of Propaganda, a man, any man, any little man who goes on thinking with his own head, imperils public order." Don Benedetto is spied on, another—more politically minded—priest obtrudes even into his home. This Don Piccirilli, who has just written an article "The Scourge of Our Time," is a fine satirical foil to the saintly, bold old man.

"'Was it about the war and unemployment?' asked Don Benedetto.

This remark annoyed Don Piccirilli.

"'Those are political questions,' he answered. 'Only spiritual questions are dealt with in the diocesan journal. From the purely spiritual point of view, the scourge of our time, in my opinion, is immodesty of dress.'"

Don Benedetto turns over the essays his pupils had written for him at college, and he compares the naïve genuine aspirations in those essays with the careers their authors are now following: careers of municipal and party graft and intrigue, and the novel is an attempt to answer Don Benedetto's question as to what obscure and pitiless destiny had played havoc with their generation, so that his most promising pupil, the only one who has retained his love of humanity, his honesty and charity, is an outlaw from the State and the Church.

I wish I could convey the poetry, the pity and clarity, of this novel. Signor Silone is a master of vivid images (the old peasant woman's hands crossed on her breast "looked like two old utensils worn out by long and painful labour") and of a bitter and truthful humour (Spina discussing a Socialist leaflet on the Abyssinian war says, "It might have been written on purpose to rouse the sympathies of the masses in favour of the war, which it describes as a robber's enterprise. If we succeed in convincing the unemployed that there really is anything to steal in Abyssinia, many of them will promptly enlist."). He has many of the qualities of a major novelist, and the criticisms of so honest and Christian a writer deserve to be read with patience and sympathy by Catholics. Perhaps I should add that this novel is hardly suitable for the immature reader.

All the novels on my list are concerned with social justice, and they all avoid the merely political approach. The trouble is: what approach can you have but the political or the religious? However objectively you write, you cannot avoid criticism, and to criticise, you must compare. The strength of Signor Silone is that he writes—as "a disappointed lover"—from a religious angle: he has a basis for comparison if not in the Church of today, which in his view tolerates cruelty and injustice, then in the Church of yesterday. Mr. Calder-Marshall and Mr. Masefield both deal with social injustice, both are novelists too truthful to see their drama in black and white, in terms of good Socialist and bad Capitalist, but Mr. Masefield's "baselessness" is the cause of some sentimentality in his story of a Socialist baker in a country town who is ruined by his protest in court against what he considers an unjust sentence (a mad boy is, rather improbably, sentenced to death for the murder of a keeper in which he was unwittingly concerned). Mr. Masefield criticizes—one may imagine his claiming—from the side of common humanity, but he doesn't recognize, as Signor Silone expressly does, that that is to take sides with the weak, the evil, the cankered, the fallen. None the less, Mr. Masefield's novel can be warmly recommended: his narrative style is admirably plain and unpretentious, and certain incidents, the boys' improvised bull-fight in a farmer's field and the opening by the baker's son and wife of a dreadful little refreshment room for factory workers in an industrial city, are as vivid as anything Mr. Masefield has written. The happy ending on the last three pages is so absurd that it has a kind of fairy-tale charm.

Mr. Calder-Marshall, too, has done nothing better than some sections of *Pie in the Sky*. His style since *About Levy* has richly matured: it has lost its dryness and abruptness: he has allowed a sensuous appeal to steal in (a sign of confidence and strength). But I do not think he has yet found a satisfactory technique, and a certain weakness and diffusion in his new novel is due partly to the same "baselessness" we have noticed in Mr. Masefield and partly to his "panoramic" method, the arrangement in short sections of several different plots, which only in some cases a little overlap. The Victorian novelists, too, were fond of a sub-plot, but it is impossible to read, say, *Middlemarch*, without feeling the interest slacken whenever we leave the main characters. For the single sub-plot, Mr. Calder-Marshall substitutes half a dozen, but he has so enlisted our interest in the characters of the ranker Capitalist and his two sons, that we resent interruptions, even when they contain so superb a comic figure as Mr. Robinson, shady go-between of shady clients. A less important error, to my mind, is the way in which workshop scraps have been left lying about, touches of parody in Joyce's manner, and two or three passages of mental monologue in italics, which could only be justified if they formed part of the general method. (The trouble with this kind of monologue is that it is too easy: it avoids all the exciting and refreshing difficulties of dramatization.) But enough of complaint. Let me quote two passages to show the speed and wit of his style, his imaginative symbolism: the description of a mean house in which a man is dying of consumption—"Any of the windows might have been marked in the photograph with a white cross (X), where the corpse was found. Any of the furniture had enough idiosyncratic ordinariness to look vivid in the Chamber of Horrors"; of a state of mind—"Now he saw himself more clearly, as a person of great importance to himself, of lesser and lessening importance to friends and acquaintances, a useful enemy, a cipher to strangers, a foreigner to Frenchmen."

February 20th, 1937
Fiction Chronicle

The Porch. By Richard Church. Dent. 7s. 6d.
Delicate Monster. By Storm Jameson. Ivor Nicholson & Watson. 5s.
War with the Newts. By Karel Capek. Translated by M. and R. Weatherall. Allen & Unwin. 7s. 6d.
By-Road. By Adrian Bell. Cobden-Sanderson. 7s. 6d.

For seventeen years until 1933, Richard Church worked as a customs and excise officer in a laboratory under Tower Bridge in London; his job was to test samples of tea, cocoa, chocolate and egg-yolk, an experience that informed his novel *The Porch* (1937), the first in a trilogy of fictions about the British Civil Service. Greene was put off by the novel's slow-moving pace and the "universal kindliness" of its characters (*The Porch* is dedicated, rather tweely, to 'The Administrative and The Executive of our Civil Service, who Together Comprise a Treasury of Good Fellows'), yet he praised the author's "unpretentious distinction". The Yorkshirewoman Storm Jameson, notoriously hot-tempered, wrote over forty-seven novels; Greene especially enjoyed *Delicate Monster* for its "mental atmosphere of jealousy", though it is not known if he met Jameson, who died in 1972 at the age of ninety-five. The Czech author Karel Capek had introduced the word "robot" into the English language (the title of his 1920 play being *Rossum's Universal Robots*), and much of his work has a science fiction flavour. *War with the Newts*, outwardly a fantasy, was intended to warn against Hitler's drive to acquire living-space in the East. ("Hello, you humans. No need for alarm", announce the newts of the title. "We have no hostile intentions towards you. We need only more water, more coasts, more shallows to live in.") Adrian Bell's 1930 novel of Suffolk country life, *Corduroy*, was a bestseller that encouraged hundreds of city-dwellers to take up farming (even if they had never aspired to farming). His sixth novel, *By-Road*, unfolds amid the Suffolk fruit-growing business and failed to excite Greene. In 1929, by a coincidence, Bell's Suffolk house 'Seabrooks' had been turned into a pub by Graham Greene's family firm—Greene King brewers.

"For all would waste a Stoic's heart"—this phrase from Donne stands as epigraph to Mr. Church's novel. His modern Stoic is Quickshott, a young man who, in the first chapter, enters the big Georgian Custom House in Thames Street to take up his duties as a Civil Servant in the Food and Drugs Analysis Department. It is an admirable opening to a novel written throughout with unpretentious distinction: it recalled to me that other scene in much the same neighbourhood, when Conrad's young Powell dared the catacombs of the Shipping Office with his mate's certificate ("That day I wouldn't have called the Queen my cousin"), but a gulf separates the enthusiastic young seaman from the lonely Quickshott, with his medical and philosophical ambitions and his Board School education, who is simply achieving security in the safest Service in the world. What recalls Conrad, I suppose, is the vivid and emotive images from common life, for undoubtedly the most vital scenes in Mr. Church's novel are set in the sample rooms, amid "the sleepy roar of the muffle-furnace and the sighing of the bunsens; the slapping and leaping of the distillates boiling in the flasks," where in the wine-test room the master-instrument floats in pure alcohol, a beautiful golden instrument catching the light in its cylinder of liquid.

Mr. Church's discreet and subtle expression does not directly disclose his theme, but I take it to be Quickshott's gradual discovery, through pain and error, that it is the Service he has entered for material reasons which will most satisfy his unfledged stoicism. He rebels at first against the unintelligent routine, but it is not that dull discipline which is to cause him most waste of heart: it is the world outside, his private ambitions and affections, in particular the responsibility he undertakes for his friend and colleague, the sick, embittered poet Mouncer. "You have got to learn," his superior tells him, "what is expected of you in the Service. A Civil Servant is like a soldier or a sailor. He must work without thought of himself. He can have as many private ambitions and activities as he likes; but he must be prepared to drop them at a moment's notice when called upon by the necessity of his office. And he must work anonymously, without expecting reward or even notice," and in another passage the same speaker refers to Civil Servants as "true Stoics." The conception may seem similar to that of the totalitarian state, but there is this enormous difference: it is not a universal immolation, but an immolation of the few for the many. Quickshott, the romantic, cherishes a phrase of Epictetus: "Here is a great thing to say: 'I am he who ought to take care of mankind,'" but he rebels against the Service discipline, believing it more important to save an individual. Mouncer wastes Quickshott's energies and dies, and Quickshott fails in the examination which was to be his first step towards release from the Service.

It would be interesting if one had the space to compare this genuinely philosophic novel with books like *The Fountain* and *Sparkenbroke*[5]. No one in *The Porch*, any more than in *The Fountain*, reads anything lighter than *John Inglesant*[6]: "He had no time even to select a book to take with him, and at the last minute he snatched up a copy of Jevon's *Logic*"; but how differently that would sound in Mr. Morgan's aristocratic and brocaded pages. It is men of Quickshott's class who really have to snatch at Jevon's *Logic*: they are driven, constricted and disciplined by poverty. The philosophical ideas in Mr. Morgan's novels ineffectually decorate and disguise the plot itself: the old novelette situations, an absorption in themes of no more dignity than whether A will eventually "get" B. Mr. Church's novel is unlikely to please so large a public, for he ignores the suspense-value of the double bed, and though he does not altogether avoid, in his portrait of the poet, the romantic and melodramatic element which nearly always creeps in when the private eccentricity of genius is given public form, he justifies, better than Mr. Morgan, the bold act of printing some of the poems.

What I found a little antipathetic in Mr. Church's novel was the universal kindliness of his characters: even Quickshott's chiefs have more bark than bite, and some of his private friends, the whimsical Mr. Finch in particular, seem to be carefully composed bundles of rather literary "humours". Not one has the reality of Quickshott himself or the vividness of the sample beers and the bunsen burners of the Department.

Miss Jameson's characters, on the other hand, are immediately acceptable. How one's heart warms to Dr. Johnson when he replies to the lady who asks him if no man is naturally good: "No, madam, no more than a wolf." And so it does to Miss Jameson for this long-short story full of malice, expressed with invigorating plainness. (Perhaps I should add that the story is not for convent schools.)

Delicate Monster is a vivid study of a popular and romantic actress (though I do not think we are meant seriously to believe that she is an *actress*), written by the wife of one of the many men she has seduced. "When she has a love affair she takes care that the details shall be known to as many persons as possible, so that posterity can have no excuse for a mistake. When she reads a severe notice of her acting, she puts it down to envy. She does not understand that an envious critic may be telling the truth, since envy, hatred and malice are among the motives that prompt critics to be honest."

There are two strands to this very simple tale: the jealousy of the narrator (I cannot recall any other living writer who has so convincingly, unexaggeratedly and horrifyingly described the mental atmosphere of jealousy: it deserves to be remembered with Swann's unhappy passion for Odette) and the relation between the actress and her daughter whom she brings up, dramatizing herself as the understanding mother, more friend than parent, to become a fleshly romantic after her own style. "She was never checked for using a gross word. When she came home in the holidays, Victoria engaged a governess, who had the strictest orders not to put ideas of religion or modesty into the child's head." As the girl remarks, when she reacts from the D.H. Lawrence environment and "blood-consciousness:" "I couldn't stand being understood by mamma ... You can't call a single nasty thought your own after Mamma has gone through your mind." The girl marries simply, sentimentally and happily, and has from the first to fight her mother, who tries by every trick in her power to break the marriage, to get her child to conform to her own romantic and adulterous standards. But the age has changed: "blood-consciousness" is a stale gambit: it is the daughter who wins.

This is not a new book of Miss Jameson's. It was published on the Continent some time ago. But nothing she has written has stood the test of time so well. Hatred and malice have certainly made for honesty: there isn't a bogus sentence in the book. A subject which could easily be treated hysterically is treated with a kind of common sense which is close to the poetic. "What is more ridiculous than a deceived wife? They sing comic songs about her ... The stages of her grotesque agonizing experience are squeezed between two phrases – 'jealousy is as hard as the grave' and 'Are you going to tell your missus when you get ho-ome, who you were with last night?'" We believe in this agony, as we are unwilling to believe in the mental storms of Lawrence's characters, just because Miss Jameson never makes an exaggerated claim. "What I went through that night numbed some part of my mind. I have felt nothing so acutely since. (Here I should add that nothing can be sillier than to compare agony of mind with severe physical agony. The worst of the former is easier to put up with than the second. A torn mind is pleasure to a torn stomach—even the after-pains of an abdominal operation are worse than being made a fool of, in the most humiliating manner in the world, by a husband or a lover.)"

I have no room to do more than warmly recommend Mr. Capek's fantasy of a world conquered by newts, a story reminiscent of the early Wells, but with more wit and less horror, and Mr. Bell's study of a fruit farmer with new ideas who revolutionizes the old, slow, Suffolk way of life. Mr. Bell has returned to the plain style of *Corduroy*, and those of us to whom the influence of Lamb never seems other than disastrous will welcome the change.

March 27th, 1937
Fiction Chronicle

Theatre. By W. Somerset Maugham. Heinemann. 7s. 6d.
The Fleshly Screen. By Edward Dodge. Faber and Faber. 7s. 6d.
The Bachelor of Arts. By R.K. Narayan. Nelson. 7s. 6d.
Dinosaur Tracks. By Benedict Thielen. Secker & Warburg. 7s. 6d.
Juan in China. By Eric Linklater. Jonathan Cape. 7s. 6d.

In choosing to write about espionage in a mood of disenchantment and prosaic reality, Somerset Maugham anticipated the modern spy thriller. Appropriately Greene included Maugham's short story "The Hairless Mexican", in his 1957 anthology of spy literature, *The Spy's Bedside Book*, and by his own admission was indebted to his famous plain style and storytelling powers. Greene knew Maugham slightly (he was with Maugham in the lounge of Claridge's when King Edward VIII made his historic abdication speech), and made a point of reviewing him in *The Spectator* and elsewhere. *Theatre*, an English version of Colette's thespian novel *Chéri*, is a romance about an ageing actress and her young lover. Maugham had worked in the theatre for thirty years and knew his material so well that the novel occasionally reads like reportage. It came out in March 1937 in a print run of 20,000 copies; Greene loved it. R. K. Narayan had worked (very briefly) as a teacher, then as a journalist, before publishing his first novel, *Swami and Friends* (1935). The novel introduced the imaginary small town of Malgudi in southern India, which Narayan was to map out and populate in succeeding novels, including *The Bachelor of Arts*, which Greene helped to publish. Benedict Thielen, now forgotten, was an American short story writer and star contributor to *The New Yorker*. Greene admired Thielen, though not, however, Eric Linklater, whose novel *Juan in China*, set in Shanghai during the outbreak of the Sino-Japanese War in 1937, he found an irritatingly "Linklaterian" melange of hilarity and grotesque farce. ("As a fantasy it carries too heavy a load to soar", Greene judged.) Edward Dodge has fallen off the map of English literature.

There could hardly be a greater contrast than that between Mr. Maugham's carnal, savage and cosmopolitan chronicle and Mr. Dodge's gentle poetic evocation of *Temps Perdu* in a provincial city. Perhaps the contrast between their methods, the story recorded as it happens in the crudity and vividness of the moment, and the story remembered can best be described in Boswell's words: "I also think that even harsh scenes acquire a softness by length of time; and many scenes are like very loud sounds, which do not please till you are at a distance from them, or at least do not please so much; or like strong coarse pictures, which must be viewed at a distance, and I don't know how it is, but even pleasing scenes improve by time, and seem more exquisite in recollection, if they have not faded to dimness in the memory. Perhaps there is so much evil in every human enjoyment when present, so much dross mixed with it, that it requires to be refined by time."

Mr. Dodge's novel, like one of Turner's later pictures, is all air and light. It belongs to recollection. Mr. Maugham's belongs to the harsh immediate moment: here are the loud sounds and the strong coarse pictures. His method is more obviously contemporary. Infinitely more civilized it yet belongs to the same tradition as Hemingway and the American "tough" writers. What, of course, he possesses is a gift of salty cultivated and critical phrase quite beyond them: "He was thin and rather small, with a lined face and close-cropped white hair. His features had a worn distinction. He reminded you of a head on an old coin that has been in circulation too long." His new novel, although its subject may seem a rather worn one—the careers of successful actresses, if we can believe the writers of fiction, usually end on the gigolo note, the struggle to retain youth, a lover, passion, and the rest of it—is told in that plain, straightforward, commonsense manner which always, in Mr. Maugham's work, cunningly disguises uncomfortable depths of irony, a complete disbelief in human nature. The implications of so apparently casual a phrase as: "her own career had been singularly lacking in hardship" are immense. Julia Gosselyn, the faded energetic and highly-sexed "great" actress: Tom Fennell, the accountant young enough to be her son with whom for a time she is in love and whose intricate knowledge of how to bilk the Income Tax authorities makes him welcome in every County family: Avice, Fennell's girl, an actress of dreadful refinement and incompetence: they hardly show human nature at its romantic best, but how refreshing in a period of Left-Wing heroics, of the noble shock troops increasing the output of golosh factories in the cause of international Communism, and dying on foreign soils, in *B.O.P.*[7] fashion, clasping the Red Flag, to read of the shabbier passions, the less noble ideals, to have a pleasantly astringent dose of Original Sin.

Mr. Dodge's story is of enviable simplicity: a boy in a provincial town, his board school education, his first sentimental approach to sex, the love which condemns him for life to a dreary job in a drapery, the not-quite happiness of a not-quite suitable marriage: emotions too real to be given such a blatant adjective as tragic. Reading *The Fleshly Screen*, one realizes how often in a novel subject is lost in plot, the immense difficulty of controlling the incidents, of retaining the simplicity of the first idea. The first idea: with most people, I suppose that is the one enjoyable moment in creation. Then the plot begins: the depressing struggle to keep the extraneous characters off the page; and half the sense of poetry in this novel comes simply from that: it has never lost the subdued excitement of the primary moment. More even, I think, than from the curious idealized, and yet emotionally accurate, observation, always safely this side of sentimentality, which catches the very feel of the seasons, of night and day, of dark provincial evenings and the smell of candles at early services; the oars creaking on the river on summer evenings, brass bands on Sunday mornings, playing under the limes: the nostalgia for past time.

I hope the fact that I have written an introduction to Mr. Narayan's second novel[8] does not debar me from recommending it here. It is a novel of the very finest promise: the story of a young Indian in his last year at a college in Mysore and during his first year of freedom. Humorous, and oddly poignant, it has a great deal in common with the stories of Tchehov: the same almost grotesque vividness in the characterization, the same underlying sense of beauty and sadness; the huge Indian distances into which friends disappear to take up little official jobs and never to write letters; fine plans and great ambitions narrowing down under the pressure of life. But the book, I think, will be popular for its humorous surface: for Natesan, the college union secretary, who bribes his way to office with coffee and tiffin; Gajapathi, the Professor of English, who finds errors in Fowler and corrects Bradley on Shakespeare; the holy thief who steals flowers to lay before the Gods; Kailas, the sentimental and drunken debauchee ("mother is a sacred object. It is a rare commodity, sir. Mother is a rare commodity"); the hero, Chandran, always drawing up detailed time-tables for living and always finding them disarranged by this and that, a visit to the cinema, the sight of a girl by the riverside. It is one of those rare books one can recommend unreservedly to every class of reader.

Mr. Thielen will be well-known to readers of *The New Yorker*. His short stories are sophisticated and streamlined; they catch appearances with some of the ease, if not all the implications, of Miss Sally Benson's: appearances which belong to the rather loud, naïve and brutal American scene; to Rotarian breakfast clubs, drummers honeymooning in painted deserts, the culture hunt of tourists in

Florence, to sudden inexplicable atrocities. The following description of American women bargain-hunting gives some measure of Mr. Thielen's talent:

> "They went out of the restaurant and headed for the clothing department. As they got out of the elevator and were suddenly surrounded by dresses, skirts and coats, a complete change came over both their faces. Their faces became suddenly hard and eager and their bodies tense, like the trembling tense bodies of hunting dogs when they are on the scent. They looked quickly about, trying to take in everything that was there at once. Their eyes had a cold distant look in them, as though they were ready for unexpected cruelties. They even almost forgot the children that clung to their arms. At first they went in opposite directions, but they soon came together, Mrs. Mason and Mrs. Hoag meeting mid-way, each with two flowered chiffon dresses marked down to seven ninety-eight, clutched by their hangers and flowing softly after them. They made for a mirror, getting there a split second before a young and (they were certain) immoral person who was coming from the opposite direction. They held the dresses alternately up in front of them, turning their heads sideways to look at the effect. Junior began to puff up and down the length of the room, imitating a train and occasionally running into someone, but they hardly noticed him. Now and then they darted to a new rack of dresses and thumbed them over like the leaves of a book in which there is a certain passage which has suddenly become terribly important to find."

I must confess myself to be in a minority on the subject of Mr.

Linklater's humour. I infinitely prefer his *Men of Ness*, where the gusto, which is the chief characteristic of his style, has more natural play in dragon-ships and wassails and Viking blood-letting: more natural because less controlled by prudence. As a humorist he is incurably "naughty," without ever risking the charge of immorality. Mr. Linklater writes for a big family public, and his Rabelaisianism always stops short of a blush. Words, words, words: that is the chief impression left by the adventures of his modern Don Juan in an embattled China. And since Mr. Linklater has too much good taste to consider the plight of those people under the fire of the Japanese machine-guns a fit subject for humour, *Juan in China* lurches uncomfortably from the naughty to the adventurous, from the adventurous to quite serious-minded, though still wordy, satire. As a fantasy it carries too heavy a load to soar.

NOTES

1. Most people refer to Green (being French-born) as Julien. However, it used to amuse Green to use both spellings of his name, depending on which language he was using; English editions of his books mostly use "Julian"; French, "Julien".

2 In his book *The English Novel* (1929), Ford Maddox Ford accused Fielding and Thackeray of being "horrible bad constructors of plots"; the Fielding-Thackeray tradition of the English novel represented, in Ford's estimation, "the nuvvel", which was really the literature of escape.

3. Gerhardie's original surname was Gerhardi, but he added a final "e" towards the end of his life apparently because other great writers—Shakespeare, Blake—had a final "e". In 1972 Greene wrote to Gerhardie: "It's very difficult to compress one's admiration [of your work] into so short a space, but alas I am struggling with a novel [*The Honorary Consul*] which won't come right and I haven't the energy to write properly on your work as I would wish. You know how much I have always admired it."

4. *A Christmas Garland (Woven by Max Beerbohm)* was published in 1912, with Beerbohm's parodies of Henry James, G. K. Chesterton, Hilaire Belloc and Joseph Conrad.

5. *The Fountain* (1932) and *Sparkenbroke* (1936) were novels by *The Times* drama critic Charles Langbridge Morgan.

6. *John Inglesant*, a celebrated historical novel by Joseph Henry Shorthouse (1834-1903), set amid 17th century religious intrigue in England and Italy.

7. *B.O.P.*: *Boy's Own Paper.*

8. Greene is referring to Narayan's *Bachelor of Arts* (1937).

five

INTERVIEWS AND TRIBUTES

23 September 1989

WHY I AM STILL A CATHOLIC
Graham Greene on God, sex and death

An Interview by John Cornwell

Greene claimed to be unhappy with John Cornwell's interview, and complained to Tom Burns: "I rather rashly gave permission to *The Tablet* to syndicate the interview because I thought that Cornwell's book on the death of John Paul I [*A Thief in the Night*] was excellent. I regretted it later." Cornwell, a distinguished journalist and now a Cambridge scholar, had made a few (extremely minor) errors, which irritated Greene. "I have two armchairs and not one, and I have never drunk a vodka cocktail in my life. It would have been pure virgin vodka!" Nevertheless, the interview proved to be a literary sensation. Not to be outdone by *The Tablet*, the London *Times* published a detailed summary of "Why I am still a Catholic" on the very day it appeared in the Catholic journal. By granting *The Tablet* "intimate access to his own private life", the newspaper surmised, Greene must be "repaying a long-term debt of gratitude for an ancient favour". *The Times* went on to describe Greene as a "rather nice kind gentleman,

Graham Greene with his French companion Yvonne Cloetta in Tomsk, USSR, 1987.

very old and very modern, very graceful and scandalous, very problematical." It concluded that *The Tablet*'s "rare, extensive and personal interview with the greatest English novelist today" was a

> literary event of some considerable interest, a terrific scoop... Greene is a Trustee of the Catholic magazine and this is not the first time he has let it use the connection. It is appropriate, for John Cornwell, the interviewer, speaks the Catholic shorthand needed to pry some of Graham Greene's sexier [*sic*] secrets from him. Some will even call it a confessional statement, though there is no plea for absolution at the end— by 85, it seems, the shame with the libido has all burnt out.

The interview took place on the eve of the collapse of Communism, when east Europeans were returning to the rosary and the Virgin Mary in their thousands. Greene was aware of the political implications behind Marian apparitions, as the Virgin had appeared routinely to a group of children in Medjugorje, Yugoslavia, since 1981. In *The Tablet* John Cornwell would express his misgivings about these visitations. The Medjugorians (he wrote in the 7 April 1990 edition) were conceivably hallucinating in a powerful act of the "religious imagination". Cornwell did not discount the possibility, either, that the children were open to exploitation—maybe even hypnosis—from impresarios of the cult. (One such, an American tour operator told him: "I think Our Lady is keeping the visions going so we can get market penetration", which comes close to simony or the sin of making money out of holy objects.) *Pravda*, likewise, would condemn sightings of the Virgin in the Ukraine as the work of nationalist extremists bent on undermining *perestroika*. (By a coincidence, the Ukrainian Mary usually appeared in a glow of orange and blue light, the Ukraine national colours.) In conversation with Cornwell, Greene says he does not care for "Mariolatry" (Virgin Mary veneration), yet he admits to saying a "Hail Mary" whenever the plane leaves the ground.

At some level, then, like the children of Medjugorje, Greene believed in the efficacy of Mary's intercession. Greene also makes much of his meeting in Italy in 1949 with the Franciscan friar Padre Pio. Then Italy's most publicized holy man, Pio was said to suffer the stigmata and was already known for his sanctity (and anti-Communism) when Greene attended his Mass with his lover Catherine Walston in Apulia, southern Italy. Typically for a novelist who was drawn to everyday wonders, Greene was less impressed by Father Pio's supernatural wounds than by the occurrence of a very "ordinary" miracle. After the priest's Mass was over, Greene looked at his wrist watch to find that almost two hours had passed, when he could have sworn that the service had lasted thirty-five minutes. In Greene's superstitious universe, causeless events did not exist, and the time-slip was evidence, he believed, of supernatural intervention. Francesco Pio was proclaimed a saint in 2002.

At the time of *The Tablet* interview Greene had a year and a half left to live.

✳   ✳   ✳

Tablet notice:
Graham Greene now calls himself a "Catholic agnostic". John Cornwell went to Antibes to find out what Greene's religion means to him.

The apartment was tiny, modest; his living room floodlit with Mediterranean sun from the sliding balcony window. There was just room for a cane sofa with cushions, and a matching armchair; a table covered with a simple cloth served as a desk. There were bookshelves with rows of Nelson and Oxford Classics, and other books, well-worn, but meticulously displayed, among them the distinctive covers of the works of Hans Küng[1]. There were several pictures on the walls, exclusively, I judged, of sentimental value.

It might have been the temporary lodging of a celibate schoolmaster, or a priest; the brownish striped wallpaper seemed institutional; not one item betrayed the wealth, the distinction, or even the good taste of its occupant—except perhaps those books.

Traffic roared in the street below. The sound of aircraft indicated the proximity of the flight path to Cannes.

"I normally keep this open, but I'll shut it for your machine", said Greene, pulling the window to.

Then he sat down immediately on the cane sofa and faced me, hunched, as if a trifle apprehensive; there was a hint of the confessional about the proceedings.

"Why", I asked, "here?" I nodded towards the forest of masts in Antibes harbour. "Were there tax advantages?"

He began to laugh breathily.

"No, no. I came to live here so as to be near to the woman I love. I have a girlfriend, a friendship of some 30 years. She is married, to a Swiss husband; but he is ... *complaisant*. All parties are in agreement. My friend and I usually have lunch together; spend the afternoon together."

Since we had sat down the years had somehow vanished from him. His skin seemed to glow with health. His hearing was clearly impeccable; his eye-sight penetrating.

"You are perhaps the most famous Catholic layman alive ...", I began. "But what sort of a Catholic *are* you? Do you go to church? Do you go to confession? Do you even *believe?*"

"I call myself now a Catholic *agnostic*", he snapped. There was no petulance; but his lips seemed to implode with the emphatic force of the words.

"I go to Mass usually on a Sunday", he went on. "I've got a great friend, a priest from Spain, Fr Leopoldo Durán, who has permission from his bishop to say the Mass in Latin and say it anywhere, so if he comes here he says it at that table. And if I'm travelling with him, he'll say Mass in the hotel room … although only on a Sunday. And to please Fr Duran I make a confession now—of about two minutes; although I've nothing much to confess at the age of 85; and I take the host then, because that pleases him. There's plenty in my past to confess, which would take a long time, but there's nothing in my present because of age. And lack of belief is not something to confess. One's sorry, but one wishes one could believe. And I pray at night … that a miracle should be done and that I *should* believe."

"Did you ever relish confession?" I asked. "In the days when you *had* something to tell?"

"Not much." He paused. "I once had a little quarrel in the confessional box. What made the whole business of confession endurable was that you only told the sins that you committed since your *last* confession. I used to go to a Carmelite church in London. I said to the priest: 'It's three months since my last confession, Father.' Then he began to ask me questions about two or three years before and had I done this or that, and I said: 'I *told* you—it's three months since my last confession. And I'm wasting *your* time, and I'm wasting *my* time, and goodbye, Father!' And I went along to the Jesuits and confessed in two minutes."

As he repeated the words with which he had quelled the priest, his voice was suddenly cold, withering.

"You became a convert to Catholicism more than 60 years ago …"

"A *sort* of convert", he corrected me promptly. "The woman I wanted to marry at that time *was* a Catholic and a very practising Catholic against the will of her mother, and I thought I should at least understand what she believed in even if I didn't believe in it myself. Therefore I took instructions from a Fr Trollope and then became convinced that at any rate this might be nearer the truth than the other religions of the world."

"The path to Catholicism is often a quest for greater certainty, a clearer authority. Were you also looking for something like that?"

"I was much more interested in the theological *arguments*. I read a good deal of theology during that period: I thought that the arguments for Catholicism were more convincing than those of other religions."

"Which theological writers influenced you?"

"Newman, von Hügel, Unamuno. And I like Frank Morrison's book *Who Moved the Stone?*[2] I liked Unamuno's spirituality; and especially his book on Cervantes. I enjoyed reading that more than *Don Quixote* itself. I also love Unamuno's *The Tragic Sense of Life.*"

"But what do you believe now? I'm wondering how a Greene catechism might read?"

He was looking at me directly, warily.

"You say you take the host to please Fr Duran. But do you *believe* in communion—the Real Presence in the Eucharist?"

"I believe in it as a commemoration of what I think happened at the Last Supper. A *commemoration*. Not necessarily to be taken literally."

Every word was precisely enunciated. He was looking at me defiantly, I thought.

"There are places in Africa", he went on, "where there is no idea even of *bread* in our sense, and no means to make or acquire it. How can one be too literal, too dogmatic, about the way in which the Eucharist is understood?"

"You talk about having had plenty to confess in your own past life. But did you actually *believe* in sin in a theological sense?"

"I've always rather disliked the word sin", he said promptly. "It's got a kind of professional, dogmatic ring about it. Crime, I don't mind the word crime, but the word sin has got a kind of priestly tone. I believe that one does something *wrong* ... and it may be a little wrong and it may be a big wrong. I never liked that strict division of mortal sin and venial sin in the Catholic Church. And then again, it depends on the consequences; some apparent little wrongs can cause more pain than apparent big wrongs. It depends on the circumstances and human relations."

"Your characters are often trapped between their weaknesses and their consciences. Do you think that temptation, a sense of guilt, adds to the spice of life?"

"No. I'd rather be without it."

"And what about Satan? Do you believe in the devil, or in demons?"

Greene smiled wanly. "No. I don't think so."

"Do you believe in angels?"

A chuckle. "No, I *don't* really."

"Do you believe in hell?"

"I don't believe in hell. I never *have* believed in hell. I think it's contradictory. They say that God is mercy ... so it's contradictory. I think there may be *nullity*, and for others something that is conscious. But I don't believe in hell and I feel that purgatory may happen in *this* life, not in a future life."

"By nullity you mean annihilation?"

"Yes. Hell is suffering; but nullity is not suffering."

"And who would deserve this nullity?"

"People like Hitler ... he would be wiped out."

"And what about yourself? Are you optimistic about your own survival beyond death?"

"Well, I would love to believe in it. And there *is* a mystery somehow. And one would like to let it be more than this world."

"Do you fear death?"

"No, and especially now ... I'd like it to come quickly. What I fear is lingering illness. I had cancer of the intestine ten years ago. I assumed that that would be that, so I wrote a number of letters and tried to arrange things in a nice way as far as I could without mentioning why. But I didn't feel any fear of death."

"And what about heaven?"

"I couldn't conceive what heaven could be. If it exists it's an entity I can't visualise in any way. My idea of heaven would be that it would be something active, rather than happiness with people one had loved, a form of activity in which we could influence life on earth ... perhaps one's prayers in that state could influence somebody on earth."

He paused for almost half a minute before adding: "I think that an inactive heaven is rather a sense of boredom."

"It's difficult to imagine", I ventured, "any kind of human existence without one's body and personal memories ..."

"Yes", he intervened swiftly, "and if one had that one would want to make use of it."

"I suppose one's ideas about heaven depend on one's notion of God. How do you think about God?"

He fell silent. For a moment his eyes looked strangely shifty, haunted.

"Do you contemplate God in a pure, disembodied way?" I asked.

"I'm afraid I don't", he said flatly.

"You think of God as Christ?"

"Yes, more ... yes, that's closer to it."

"It sounds as if belief is a struggle for you."

He sat musing for a while. "What keeps me to ... it's not strong enough to be called *belief* ... is St John's gospel, it's almost a reportage, it might have been done by a good journalist, where the beloved disciple is running with Peter because they've heard that the rock has been rolled away from the tomb, and describing how John manages to beat Peter in the race ... and it just seems to me to be first-hand reportage, and I can't help believing it ... I know that St Mark is supposed to be the earliest gospel, but there's just the possibility of St John's gospel having been written by a very old man, who never calls himself by name, or says 'I', but does describe this almost funny race, which strikes me as true."

"Don't you think there's a rational basis for a belief in God? Or the after-life?"

Greene looked down for a brief moment into his lap, unsmilingly. Then he began to chuckle breathily with raised shoulders. "That reminds me of Freddy Ayer", he said, "you know, the atheistic philosopher. He always said that given just half an hour he would convince me that there was absolutely *nothing*."

"Did you ever take him up on that?"

"No. It would have *bored* me", he said with some feeling. "Anyway, I've never really been able to understand logical positivism."

Then, after a pause: "Professor Ayer began to hedge a little towards the end. He claimed to have died for four minutes in the Fulham Road hospital[3]. But I didn't find his near-death experience all that convincing. What puzzled me was how did he know whether he had seen his great bright light *after* his heart had stopped rather than *before* his heart had stopped? In any case, after the heart stops a certain consciousness surely remains in the brain."

"You've talked in the past of having had a sort of mystical experience yourself, with Padre Pio, the Italian stigmatic. How important was that experience for your faith?"

"In 1949 I went to attend Padre Pio's Mass, in Italy, in the Gargano peninsula. I went out of curiosity. I'd heard about his stigmata. The Vatican didn't like him. A monsignor who came to have a drink with me in Rome, said: 'Oh, that holy fraud!' But he'd been examined by doctors of every faith—Jewish, Protestant, Catholic—and no faith. He had these wounds on his hands and feet, the size of a twenty-pence piece, and because he was not allowed to wear gloves saying Mass he pulled his sleeves up to try and hide them. He'd got a very nice peasant-like face, a little bit on the heavy side. I was warned that this was a very long Mass; so I went with my woman friend of that period to the Mass at 5.30 in the morning. He said it in Latin, and I thought that 35 minutes had passed. Then when I got outside the church I looked at my watch and it had been an hour and a half, or two hours, and I couldn't work out where the lost time had gone. I mean, there's always the moment of meditation after he takes the host, but he didn't seem to spend an abnormal length of time on that. And this is where I came to a small faith in a mystery. Because that *did* seem an extraordinary thing."

He sat for a while in reverie.

I said: "Do you really think that God intervenes in the affairs of man in miraculous, or mystical ways?"

Greene smiled wryly and hunched his shoulders. "Well ... I don't know. I feel it's a mystery. There *is* a mystery. There is something inexplicable in human life. And it's important because people are not going to believe in all the explanations given by the Church ... Curiously, I carry a photograph of Padre Pio in my wallet."

Greene took a well-worn wallet from his trouser pocket and fished out two small photographs. They were slightly dog-eared; sepia. As he handed them to me I detected a faint air of self-consciousness; as if, English gentleman that he was, he had been caught out in a gesture of Romish extravagance.

One depicted Padre Pio in his habit, smiling. The other showed him gazing adoringly at the host during Mass.

"Why do you keep them in your wallet like that?" I asked.

"I don't know. I just put them in, and I've never taken them out."

"When you visited Padre Pio were you looking for something at that time?"

"I may have been. During those years I was more or less attached to a woman who had great faith, and that may have influenced me to try and strengthen my own."

"And Padre Pio seems to have given you that desired stimulus …"

"Well, at any rate, it introduced a *doubt* in my *disbelief*." Greene laughed gently, an air of self-mockery.

He went on: "Padre Pio had asked for a hospital to be built, which seemed to me a remarkable request for a man who could heal people miraculously. He had a doctor friend who had come there to look after the hospital project, and that is where I stayed. It was through this doctor that I was invited to go and see Padre Pio for a personal interview in the monastery. And I refused because I said I didn't wish to change my life."

"You thought he might have made a saint of you?"

"No … but I might have lost the person I loved."

He looked up, almost a glance of mischief. Then his face became earnest.

"Padre Pio had strange powers. There was one famous case I knew of: a boy of about 16 who was in great pain with cancer. The mother went to see Padre Pio and he told her that he would take the pain on himself. The boy's pain immediately departed and during that period I heard from my friend who often visited there that at intervals during the Mass Padre Pio looked as if he was convulsed with agony. The boy eventually died, but without pain. These were stories by people who knew him and were on the spot."

"If you hadn't had your mysterious experience with Padre Pio you might possibly have lost your faith?"

"I don't think my belief is very strong; but, yes, perhaps I would have lost it altogether ..."

"Do you have a veneration for any other saint?"

"No." He looked at me directly again. "But I've always had a certain sympathy for Thomas the Doubter."

"Your faith, then, is tenuous."

"One is attracted to the *Faith*", he said with a wry smile. "Believing is the problem."

"Edith Sitwell once said that she thought you had a vocation to be a priest ..."

"I don't know whether it's true or not that she did", said Greene sceptically.

"You may not have had a priestly vocation, but you evidently like the company of priests."

"I see a lot of the Trappist monks, because when I go on my travels in Spain with my Fr Durán we always stay in a Trappist monastery in Galicia. I got to know the monks very well and they're very kind to us. Actually when I wrote *Monsignor Quixote* I divided my Spanish and Latin American royalties between these Trappists and the FMLN[4], the guerrillas in Salvador."

Greene's eyes lit up with the incongruity of the association.

"When you visit your Trappist monks, do you pray?"

"No. We talk. Being Trappists, having taken a vow of silence, they like a good gossip." Again, that mischievous smile. "They're allowed to talk when they've got visitors."

"Do you go to this monastery as a religious retreat?"

"No. For pleasure! Although I was first put off by the food I was given, because the monk on duty at that time cooked very badly. So Fr Durán and I used to pretend that we'd had dinner on our way and arrive late to avoid supper. Later they got a good cook and we had excellent meals."

"Do you wonder what it might have been like to be a monk?"

"I'm afraid I like women far too much for that." He rocked to and fro a little with mirth.

"When James Joyce portrayed the struggle between the vocations of priest and writer in *Portrait of the Artist*, he argued that the writer was pitched in rivalry against God—that the writer's instinctive attitude was '*Non serviam*'."

"I don't know that the writer is *against* God. But the writer in a sense is a little God working by instinct; for example, I've often found that the beginning of a book is very sticky and I generally know roughly the beginning and roughly the end; I know nothing about the middle, and I sometimes put in something that makes no sense whatever, it doesn't seem to help the character or action or anything else. And then perhaps a year later, as I'm approaching the end, the reason for it appears as if without knowing, by instinct, that this particular thing would be needed 150 pages along."

"Is this being *guided* by God, or being God-*like*?"

"God-*like*", Greene chuckled. "It's this ability to control the past, present and future ..." He paused for a moment, his eyes alert as if striving for a recollection. He went on: "Once in the midst of *A Burnt-Out Case* I was completely blocked and I didn't know how to go on, and on my way through Rome I had a dream which was not my own dream, it was the dream of my character; and the next day I put it into the manuscript and I became unblocked: the book went on ... Somehow there's a parallel there with the mystery of individual free will and predestination."

"You will always be remembered as a *Catholic* writer. Do you like that idea?"

"I always claim *not* to be a Catholic writer. They only *discovered* that I was a Catholic after I wrote *Brighton Rock*. I'm a writer who happens to be a Catholic. Not a Catholic writer. And that's what Paul VI meant when he told me that my books would always offend some

Catholics, and that I shouldn't pay any attention."

"Do you think that becoming a Catholic made you a better writer?"

"I think I was in revolt against the Bloomsbury School, E. M. Forster, Virginia Woolf, and I thought that one of the things that gave reality to characters was the importance of human beings with a future world: it made the characters far more important ... I found a certain flatness in the Bloomsbury circle of writers. There was something missing."

"You mentioned that Fr Durán says Mass for you in Latin? That's a bit reactionary, isn't it? Evelyn Waugh used to get priests to say Mass for him in Latin after the change-over."

"Evelyn Waugh and I were poles apart politically ... I personally found the liturgical changes irritating because I used to go in London to a small church where Mass was said in Spanish, which I couldn't speak. Under the old rite one could follow the Latin, because one had the translation in one's missal, so I was irritated in not being able to follow the Mass when it was said in a language I did not know."

"A lot of things have changed in the Catholic Church since you became a convert in 1926. Do you find the Church today more, or less, to your liking?"

"I'm very uncomfortable with the Church's teaching on contraception. I think that contraception is vital for human life. And instead of that, through the Church's teaching, you have an increase in abortions which one *is* reluctant to see; but with overpopulation in Africa and all round the world I think that contraception and planned birth is a necessity. In any case, it was quite clear that the majority of bishops under Paul VI were in favour of contraception, but he ignored it and went his own way; even though he made it clear it was his own way and it could be changed. So I'm very uncomfortable with the present Pope, who wants to enforce the old rules."

"One of your characters in *The Power and the Glory* says that the faithful should be loyal to the Church they have—rather than some ideal of a Church that does not exist."

"I've always been very keen on Newman, because he believed in the development of Christian doctrine, that the Church *can* change. It's not stuck in a rut—this is *true* and that's *untrue*."

He paused for a moment. His face seemed to cloud over. "Don't you find", he continued, "that the Roman Curia reminds you a little bit of the Politburo?" He mused for a while, before adding, with a little sigh, "But even the *Politburo* is changing."

"You once said that your relationship to the Church was that of a member of the Foreign Legion fighting for a city from which you were in exile. Does one go into exile in the desert—join the Foreign Legion—because it's impossible to live up to the high ideals of the imperial capital?"

"Ideals can be good or bad, and what I feel is that the Church at the moment is enforcing *bad* ideals. I think humanity *demands* control of birth. I wouldn't call the Church's attitude there an ideal, I would call it an *ideology*. The fatal date on this contraception doctrine is the First Vatican Council in 1870 and the introduction of infallibility ... Cardinal Newman was against infallibility. Infallibility was hedged round with certain conditions—that it must be on the subject of faith or morals and in accordance with the teaching of the Apostles. Contraception existed in the Roman Empire and there's not a word in the gospels on the subject: so infallibility shouldn't apply. The state of the world as it is ... and now with the addition of AIDS, it's a dangerous error. I think a great many priests have left the ministry because they are required to enforce this teaching when there's poverty and overpopulation, and they must begin to doubt whether they are enforcing a fair law which might begin to affect their deciding to give up."

"In *The Power and the Glory* you depicted courageous priests who faced death rather than abandon their calling. Does it depress you to see so many priests nowadays abandoning their ministries?"

"It does not depress me. I accept it as a fact, and I tend to put the blame on those who are now in authority in the Church." Greene leant forward, staring at the floor intently. "When I was with the Gurkhas in Malaya", he continued, "I met an army chaplain; after dinner I found myself alone with him. I brought up the subject, and he said: 'We're losing more people from the Church with this contraception thing than anything else.' And he said that in the confessional directly somebody started confessing about contraception he would change the subject at once and ask—'Have you done anything against charity?' That seemed to me a reasonable attitude in a priest."

Greene was now staring at me challengingly. There was a hint of combat.

"Don't you believe", I asked, "that the Catholic Church is entitled to put forward arguments from natural law?"

"Well, I think it's an *un*-natural law", he countered emphatically. "Sex is not only a question of pleasure. They run down *love*, and call it *pleasure*."

"Did you ever confess the 'sin' of contraception yourself?"

"No ... I don't think I ever confessed that", he said guardedly.

"But did you practise it during the days when it was universally regarded in the Church as a mortal sin?"

"I used to try and *manage* it", he said; a cautious note in his voice. "Because my wife was very much afraid. Her mother had made her afraid of childbirth, and at the same time I didn't want her conscience to be upset. I tried to manage things skilfully ... but a child did come in the end."

"You've been very outspoken in politics. Have you used your

position as a leading Catholic writer to affect the opinion of church leaders on birth control?"

"I had lunch alone with Cardinal John Heenan[5], at the time of Vatican II. And a friend of mine, Archbishop David Mathew, said, 'For goodness sake don't bring up contraception!' But I *did*. And I told the cardinal that I knew two Catholic girls who'd had abortions, but which they would not have had if they had been practising contraception. We talked quite a bit, and he seemed to become much more moderate in the course of our conversation. And I think I did influence him."

"From what you say, you're against abortion."

"Yes. At any rate, I'd like to see them reduce the legal number of weeks even further."

"Is there any way out of the contraception dilemma for the Church?"

"I think it could all be solved by a better Pope ..."

"Have you met John Paul II?"

"Only in my dreams, and I'm afraid my encounters have not been very happy ones."

Greene leant back on the sofa and cocked his head.

"In the summer of 1987", he went on, "I dreamt that I was reading in the newspapers that the Pope was considering canonising Jesus Christ, and I found myself thinking that the man must be *mad* with *pride* to be thinking of giving an honour to Christ ..."

"So where has this Pope gone wrong?"

"I don't think this Pope has doubt", went on Greene. "I don't think he doubts his own infallibility." He paused, shoulders hunched. "He reminds me a bit of Reagan, you know, John Paul II. He's always on television, isn't he? He's a good actor. And he wanted to *be* an actor when he was young. He needs a big crowd, or a camera crew. Gorbachov, on the other hand, reminds me much more of John

XXIII."

"John Paul lacks doubt, you say, and yet you pray to *believe*."

"In a curious way I've always believed that *doubt* was a more important thing for human beings. It's *human* to *doubt*. We're now entering a period where Marxism is being doubted by Marxists. I mean, he's no longer infallible, Marx. And the Pope is no longer infallible. And I think it's a great value, those two aspects. Isn't it lack of doubt that gives rise to fanaticism? We're seeing in Russia doubt raising its head, and we're seeing Catholics rejecting unyielding dogma ... In this sense Communism and Christianity are coming closer together; but unfortunately the present Pope is attempting to re-establish infallibility."

"Marxism nevertheless sees human nature as perfectible by social and political change alone. Isn't that a problem for Christians?"

"Don't you think that Marxists are now realising that it's *not* perfectible by *any* means?"

"Yet as a Christian", I said, "you would say that human nature is perfectible through redemption."

"I don't believe in perfectibility *any* way, on *either* side. We can improve conditions, but I don't think we can expect a perfect world. I think that Marxism began to have its own theory of infallibility, and now it's losing it."

"Is it possible to be *right*-wing and a good Christian?"

"It would be perhaps difficult." Greene chuckled to himself. "And difficult also for the complete Marxist to be a Christian."

"Have you involved yourself with liberation theology?"

"I don't like the liberation church in Managua because there's a very blood-curdling picture of the murder of Romero[6] on the wall, and there's a Christ portrayed in modern man's working clothes; and I didn't like the fact that it was all a middle-class congregation. I didn't see a single poor person in this liberation-theology church. I much prefer the awful traditional statues and a poor congregation. The poor can associate with these things.

"That's emotional, I suppose, but intellectually I like the *idea* of liberation theology—the option for the poor, and their base communities, the determination to spend time in trying to improve their situation, their *morale* rather than their *morals*."

"You've always inclined to the Left, but isn't there nevertheless something fundamentally conservative about the very *notion* of original sin?"

"I've always disliked the phrase original *sin*. I would rather say that human beings were born with certain *tendencies* for which they were not responsible. And there may be something reactionary about the current leadership of the Church, perhaps, but I don't think that applies to the Church as a whole—the priests and the people. That's the interesting thing about Archbishop Romero: he was regarded before he was made bishop as a reactionary, but immediately he was consecrated he started to attack the military and death squads; and his final sermon was an appeal to the troops to disobey orders rather than to kill. He was the only archbishop since Becket to be killed saying Mass. But he has had very little appreciation or praise in Rome."

"Since you converted to Catholicism, the Church has become more ecumenical; are *you* strongly ecumenical?"

"I'm *fairly* ... ", a short laugh, "ecumenical, yes. I think I have reservations. I don't think we can expect to be ecumenical with Muslims and Buddhists, and this, that and the other ... Or even the Jewish faith. But I'm ecumenical in the Christian communities. My daughter now attends much more an Anglican church in Switzerland."

"Does that distress you?"

"I attended a service there. There was an excellent priest who *had* been a Catholic, then he rejected Catholicism and got married and had a daughter. Then he became a parson of the local Anglican church in Menton. And I've seldom heard a better sermon. It was very thorough, and very interesting, and *short*. And my daughter much prefers it to the Catholic Church. When this man retired, the Catholic bishop came to the party that was given on that occasion." Greene snuffled to himself as if delighted with the paradox.

"You said that you were originally attracted by Catholicism because it seemed closer to the truth than any other religion. Did you feel that it was closer to the truth than any other Christian denomination?"

"Yes, I think I felt that."

"And do you still feel it?"

"But I think that it's had worse faults than some of the others. The evil side has been very evident in history. I mean Torquemada, and some of the popes. I wouldn't call the present situation evil, but I would have liked to have a John XXIV."

"Have you ever in your life attempted to convert another person to Catholicism?"

"I tried to *prevent* somebody I was very fond of. I did my best to prevent her, somebody I knew who was *tempted* to become a Catholic. And I ..." Greene had stopped, to laugh to himself. "... I managed to persuade her not to."

"Some people might think that a bit mean."

"Well, I didn't think she'd be really happier for it. She was just temporarily influenced, *too* influenced, perhaps ..."

"You have remained loyal to the Catholic Church in a public sort of way. You separated from your wife, for example, and you never divorced. But you've had long-term intimate relationships with other women."

"I have had close relationships with women for quite long periods: 12 years, 11 years, 3 years ... 30 years!" A short laugh. "They were not one-night stands, as it were. I've *had* one-night stands of course. But my friendships were relationships of a certain depth, and one kept friendship afterwards."

"You see nothing morally wrong with having mistresses?"

"It depends on the three people's point of view, if they're happy that way. Were I living with a wife I wouldn't like to have a mistress in secret, but I think it depends on the happiness of all three people."

"So you feel that your various relationships following your marriage were okay because the various parties were happy with the situation."

"I don't know that my wife was *happy* with the situation. But we got legally separated, and she made a dolls' house museum which occupied a lot of her time ... she became an authority on dolls' houses. She also has a very nice house of her own."

"You don't believe in divorce?"

"Well, *she* wouldn't have believed in divorce. And it doesn't seem necessary."

"What about an official Church annulment? Would you have considered obtaining one?"

"I think it's part of the church bureaucracy ... One trick they can play nowadays is to claim that they were practising birth control from the beginning ..." His voice trailed with a faint air of disapproval.

"How devout are you nowadays as a Catholic, in a personal way? Do you pray? Do you say an occasional 'Our Father'?"

"If you go off in an aeroplane and something begins to go wrong, you don't say an 'Our Father', you say a 'Hail Mary'. Most people do, I think. And yet even the feminists seem to be running down the stature of Mary in the Church. I automatically say a 'Hail Mary' when the plane leaves the ground. I've only had two crash-landings in my life, and I'm not afraid of aeroplanes, but I do it almost automatically."

"Do you believe in the power of prayer?"

"I *hope* that it does something." He looked tense for a moment, chortled a little to himself. "And I *do* pray ... in some detail, at night. Generally *for* people."

"Formal prayers?"

"I say a 'Hail Mary.' And then I specify ... things."

"Do you spend long praying?"

"No, five minutes perhaps."

"Do you pray the psalms?"

"The saints *bore* me. And the Old Testament ... I made fun of it in my last book. Specially Ezekiel. I like one or two hymns, quite minor poetry as it were. 'Abide With Me' I like."

"Devotion to Mary is often a stumbling block to non-Catholic Christians. Do you subscribe to a special devotion to her?"

"I don't care for *Mariolatry* very much ... But I was impressed, as it were, *politically* by the feast of the Immaculate Conception in 1985 in León, Nicaragua; because the papers were all talking about religious persecution, and it was a scene which was exactly the opposite. I went by car in the evening with Tomás Borge, the Minister of the Interior. And it was always a great feast, the Immaculate Conception, and we walked for about an hour and a half in a poor and crowded part of the city and he had only one guard with him, and in every hut there was a statue of the Virgin with candles, and the crowd would stop at each house and it was a kind of ritual; they would call out 'Who has given us happiness?' And the reply would come from the crowd—'Mary Immaculate!' And I thought this could hardly be called religious persecution. Then we moved into the rich quarter of the town and there they were celebrating, but behind closed windows and closed doors in private parties. I found it moving. But partly one was pleased politically. Nobody could call this religious persecution."

"Do you ever fear", I said provocatively, "the 'eye of the needle'?—you must be very rich." Looking round me at the modesty of his apartment I realised that my question was even more ironic than I had intended.

"I've given it all away", said Greene simply. "I'm paid a salary by a fund in Switzerland. Enough to live on. But I'm comfortable. There was a time when I had a wife and two children, and I was down to my last £20."

He was giving his snuffled laugh again. "When I realised that I was doomed to go on living forever, I felt I should let my children enjoy my money now rather than wait for it. They both have very nice houses."

"How much property do you own yourself?"

"Apart from this place I have a flat in Paris—a friend of mine lives there at present. I have a house in Anacapri, which is usually occupied: I bought that with the money I made on *The Third Man*."

"At 85, you must think of death rather often."

Greene laughed again. "I had an uncle who died at the age of 92, falling out of a tree ... he was trying to cut away a dead branch."

He sat silently for a few moments, his eyes alight with amusement. "That same uncle", he went on, "fell under a tube train at the age of 89. He was on his way to the Admiralty—where he was some kind of adviser. He survived, he told me, by keeping very still. Later on he took himself on to the meeting. He told me that the chief interest of the experience was the opportunity to view a tube train from a completely novel angle."

Still laughing, Greene rose slowly, hands on hips—as if to steady himself. "I think it's time for a drink", he said. "What can I get you?"

"Whatever *you're* having", I said.

"A vodka martini."

Two minutes later he returned from the kitchen carrying two

brimming cocktail glasses. He sat down again on the cane sofa and seemed to be encouraging one last question.

"What, in the final analysis," I said, "does your religion mean to you?"

Greene looked at me directly, wonderingly. He was raising his glass delicately to his lips. He seemed at that moment ageless; there was an impression about him of extraordinary tolerance, ripeness.

"I think … it's a *mystery*", he said slowly and with some feeling. "It is a mystery which can't be destroyed … even by the Church … a certain *mystery*."

Then he sipped his cocktail with immense relish.

13 April 1991

GRAHAM GREENE: A MEMOIR
Tom Burns

Much of this personal reminiscence would appear in Tom Burns' autobiography, *The Use of Memory*, published in 1993. Here the former editor of *The Tablet* celebrates his sixty-year friendship with Greene.

I am not sure which came first into my experience: *The Man Within* or the man himself. Graham Greene's first published novel, its title and the quotation from Sir Thomas Browne, "There is another man within me who is angry with me", at once struck a chord: one of self-recognition or the recognition of a kindred spirit, which is much the same thing. This was in June 1929. Graham was 24, I was 22.

He leapt into my landscape like a leprechaun, as it seemed to me: witty, evasive, nervous, sardonic, by turns. He was quite unlike the male company we both kept in those days, which was mainly of publishers and authors, as we joyfully joined in plans and projects. We came and went between our offices, clubs or favourite pubs in a common pursuit. Nothing was stereotyped, nothing predictable, for the world as we knew it was free—little knowing of its bondage to come.

Graham, like many young authors, was also a publisher's reader at the time. So we came to consort with his Board of Eyre & Spottiswoode. It tended to conclude its meetings at The Lamb and Flag, a pub near the Garrick. Graham seemed to me to have a spotlight on him, although his companions were by no means shadowy figures and I recall them all with affection. There was Douglas Jerrold[7], the chairman of the company, a tall, saturnine figure. He had a wound in his right arm from World War I, still preventing him from lifting a glass to his lips with ease. He was all of a Right-wing piece, the editor of a strongly conservative monthly, a vocal critic of the Bloomsbury set, a Counter-Reformation Catholic, a High and hard-headed Tory, a one-time Treasury official with a computer mind in that small head of his. In contrast was his close colleague Sir Charles Petrie, an owlish, rotund and bearded baronet, a learned historian as much at home in The Lamb and Flag as in the Carlton Club. Frank Morely made up the trio: a huge Harvard and Rhodes scholar who adopted England as his own and had settled near its heart, in Buckinghamshire, a man with all the gentleness and tolerance of a big mind and body.

In such company Graham stood out, an incurable eccentric for whom there were no comfortable assumptions. The man within was not only angry but impatient and insatiably curious. Anyway, we two seemed to hit it off. He invited me to his house on Clapham Common. Personally I was in general sceptical at that time about the possibility of any permanent matrimonial happiness and Graham's home came as a complete surprise. His gentle and beautiful wife had it all arranged with such care. There was a serenity of order in every detail: so different from everything that I had been able to observe of Graham himself. The old song of the Silver Sty came to mind: "Honey said she; Honk said he." Not that there was anything gross about Graham—he was all sensibility and courtesy—but this couple existed in two totally different circumstances in the sense that the Spanish philosopher Ortega y Gasset would say, "I am I—and my circumstance". It is an almost irremediable condition.

Paradoxically it may be cured by love which both blinds one and opens one's eyes. But Graham at the time was desperately writing, not for himself, or from any urge for self-expression, but to keep his home together. It is not surprising to read now in his published letters of this time and earlier of his passionate love and unconditional devotion for the girl he spotted in Blackwell's bookshop—as Dante spotted Beatrice at the bridge. But he was himself *and* his circumstance, with its demanding conditions. We were both much too busy to see much of each other but there would come the occasional telephone call: "Let's go to Limehouse tonight, there's a ballet of Chinese nudes at the local theatre." This sort of exultant *nostalgie de la boue* never appealed to me.

A great chance came for both of us when Graham had an instinct to write about the Mexican Revolution of President Calles and wanted to study the President's pitiless persecution of the Church at first hand. His own publisher and others were not interested: for them Mexico was far away and religion a hazy notion. Graham and I saw it quite differently and I was able to persuade my somewhat bovine Board at Longman's to accept my view and come up with £500— quite a sum in those days for a writer untried in this field. The result was all that I had hoped for: Graham's account of his tour, *The Lawless Roads*, was a graphic and devastating exposure of what he had seen. Better still, his journey gave him all the material he needed for his first breakthrough and still possibly his best novel, *The Power and the Glory*.

Unfortunately for me, Graham's regular publisher had an option on all his fiction so I could not take on the novel—but I have ever since been glad to have helped to make it possible. The "whisky priest" has become part of human experience. Many years later quite a different sort of priest with his distinct character and his own wide human appeal emerged from Graham's imagination. This was Monsignor Quixote in a book of that name. It began as a fragment and only acquired a framework in the course of writing. I was editing *The Tablet* and Graham offered a piece for a Christmas issue. He thought at the time that it would not develop into anything. But the following year came another piece: a story with a shape evolving on its own, a person emerging. But after that Graham wrote to say that he had come to a halt and would have to leave the story unfinished. I wrote to tell him that the next Christmas issue would be my last and just hoped that there would be one more instalment to mark my own finale. Graham's response was typically generous. He set to work again and virtually rounded off the story. So Monsignor Quixote was created against all odds.

It was always a stimulus to me that I had Graham's moral support and general approval throughout my editing of *The Tablet*. It was shown in innumerable ways and not least by his agreeing to become a trustee of the Tablet Trust. But to go back a bit. Just before the publication of *The Power and the Glory* came the war. We did not see or hear from each other for over five years after a brief spell together in the Ministry of Information. The break was mended with a lunch at Rules in Covent Garden. It was now my turn to introduce a wife. Our shared love of Spain and its people was apparently infectious. It infected Graham and eventually bore fruit as acknowledged by him in his dedication of *Monsignor Quixote*.

From the fifties onwards Graham and I inhabited different worlds: an occasional exchange of signals kept us in contact and some sort of contact was important to both of us. It was something like the relationship of old school friends—distanced and familiar. In our case the Church served as our Alma Mater, and some of the master we shared were Newman, von Hügel and Unamuno. Loyalty to such figures is not faith but a sort of star-wars defence system against the principalities and powers in high places where, as St Paul taught us, is the real warfare.

Some serenity came to both of us in our eighties. I recall a weekend in Antibes with him, when there was some feasting and a Mass shared in the local church while like two publicans from the Gospel we stood at the back; my eightieth birthday party at home when Graham came, to be devoured by my family and friends. It is not for me to make any judgement of anyone, but in Graham's case I shall always value his life-long resistance to all the temptations of world fame. Blessed are the poor in spirit.

A CATHOLIC TO THE LAST
John Cornwell

Here, John Cornwell takes the measure of Greene's faith and doubts. At the time of the interview Cornwell was completing his extraordinary work about the paranormal element of religion, *Powers of Darkness, Powers of Light* (1991), which Greene was sadly unable to read, being no longer alive.

In many of the tributes published and broadcast last week it was conjectured that Graham Greene had died an agnostic, estranged from the Catholic Church. One commentator remarked that he had ended his days in a state of "despair". It seems important, a week on, to begin to set the record straight.

In the summer of 1989 I went out to Antibes to interview Greene on behalf of this newspaper. In the course of two days he spent more than seven hours talking about his faith. I found him very much at peace with himself and with his Church. The word "ripeness" comes to mind.

I also found him mischievous, irreverent, eager to ride some anti-clerical hobby-horses. "Doesn't the curia remind you of the Politburo?" he asked. Later, shoulders heaving with mirth, he told me that he once dreamt that Pope John Paul II had proclaimed the canonisation of Christ.

We talked about doubt, which he seemed to regard an admirable virtue rather than an imperfection. "It is *human* to doubt", he insisted. He was contrasting doubt with infallibility, praising Gorbachev for his rejection of Communist dogma, comparing him with John XXIII. He was less sanguine about the current papacy, and utterly opposed to *Humanae Vitae*.

At one point he described himself as a "Catholic agnostic". What could he have meant? He was at pains to draw a distinction between belief and faith. "We all love the *Faith*," he said at one point, "the problem is believing in it." He did not give the impression that he was retreating from the Faith. And his inclination to believe, he said, had more recently been bolstered by reflecting on the account in John's Gospel where Peter and John raced to the empty tomb: " ... it just seems to me first-hand reportage, I can't help believing it."

There was a time, in his forties, he admitted, when he thought he might lose his belief entirely. He went to southern Italy to see Padre Pio, hoping for a miracle. During Padre Pio's Mass he found a "small faith in a mystery". The Mass seemed to last no more than thirty minutes; when he emerged from the Church, he realised that two hours had elapsed. That mysterious time-contraction was enough, he said, "to introduce a doubt into my disbelief". Down the next 40 years he kept a picture of Padre Pio in his wallet. He fished it out for me: it was dog-eared, sepia.

He said that he had recently returned to the sacraments. "I make a confession now—of about two minutes ... I take the Host then ... There's plenty in my past to confess, but there's nothing in my present because of age."

The remark confirmed the years of his "irregular status", as officialdom would put it. There had been relationships with various women; he had never sought the "bureaucratic trickery" (as he termed it) of an annulment. He felt a strong identity, it seemed, with those who languish at the margins.

He described his daily prayer. "I do pray ... in some detail, at night. Generally *for* people ..." And there were other occasions: "I automatically say a *Hail Mary* when the plane leaves the ground."

Was this symptomatic of that blend of scepticism and superstition so familiar in his fictional characters? I detected, rather, an attachment to a rugged Catholic piety. It was not a piety that smacked of anything remotely sanctimonious. Throughout our conversations he expressed a horror of casuistry, dogma, and above all religiosity.

In his younger days he had been interested in Catholic theology. In old age the details seemed to bore him. I asked him:

"Do you believe in the devil?" "No ..."

"Do you believe in angels?" "No ..."

"Do you believe in Hell?" "I don't ..."

"Do you believe in the real presence in the Eucharist?" "No ..."

"What about the after-life, heaven?"

The official view of heaven, he said, seemed "a sense of boredom". "My idea", he went on, "would be something active ... perhaps one's prayers in that state could influence somebody on earth." Again, the appeal to Catholic piety rather than to catechetics.

Before I left him for the last time, he emerged from his kitchen carrying two brimming cocktail glasses. I asked him: "What, in the final analysis, does your religion mean to you?" "I think ... it's a mystery", he said slowly and with some feeling. Then, eyeing me mischievously, he raised his glass: "It's a mystery which can't be destroyed ... even by the Church."

Catholic gentleman to the last, his loyalty, his love of the Church, had surely earned him the right to make such a quip, in good faith. May he rest in peace.

10 August 1991

GRAHAM GREENE'S WAY
Alberto Huerta

Graham Greene had described himself as a "Catholic agnostic" in his interview with John Cornwell published in *The Tablet* on 23 September 1989. What did he mean? The question is explored by an American Jesuit priest who proclaimed the gospel at the altar in Westminster Cathedral during Graham Greene's Memorial Mass in 1991.

Some critics and reviewers have always looked for ways to arrest Graham Greene's imagination and calumnise his private profession of faith. Undoubtedly they will continue to speculate on whether he was really an atheist, or a Catholic agnostic as he suggested in later years, or a true believer in the traditional and formal understanding of that term.

Responding to questions about his Catholicism in *The Other Man* (1981) by Marie-Françoise Allain, Greene makes very clear that Catholicism was a private affair for him—something not to be discussed. Yet in those conversations Greene admits:

> I'm not in opposition to Rome. I know that in my books I've introduced characters—especially priests—who verged on heresy. (That's why *The Power and the Glory* was once condemned by the Holy Office.)... I believe in the necessity of a minimum of dogmas, and I certainly believe in heresy, for it's heresy that creates dogmas. In this sense heresy has great value.

Perhaps his good friend of 27 years, Fr Leopoldo Durán, once a professor of English and American literature at the University of

Madrid, will address those detractors. But I very much doubt that Durán will write extensively about this question, even though I have urged him to do so on more than one occasion. He understood Greene as few ever did. And those of us who knew Greene primarily through correspondence soon discovered his teasingly paradoxical nature. Fr Durán will be the first to acknowledge Greene's innate sense of playfulness and intellectual provocation, in particular his raising of moral questions to prick one's conscience toward higher ethical considerations. Moreover, Durán can attest to Greene's scepticism as a useful dialectical instrument to arrive at a deeper truth. All of this is demonstrated in fictional form in the dialogues between the two friends, Monsignor Quixote and the Communist Mayor, in *Monsignor Quixote*, long and often amusing about faith, morals and politics.

My correspondence with Graham Greene began in 1982, when he published *Monsignor Quixote*. I had wanted to have something entertaining to read while on a flight from San Francisco to Rio de Janeiro, where I was scheduled to teach at the pontifical Catholic university. I picked up Greene's latest novel, hoping to break the boredom incumbent upon this long flight. Since I had written my Master's thesis on the Spanish philosopher Miguel de Unamuno (1864-1936), and had done my PhD in sixteenth-century Spanish Golden Age literature, I was interested in studying Greene's approach to Cervantes' and Unamuno's Don Quixote. Intrigued by the clever and brilliant use of the Quixote figure, I wrote to Greene for the first time ever to share with him my observations and appreciation for his ability to render a modern-day interpretation of the Quixote story. I had no idea that my letter would initiate a new friendship. A decade and 38 letters later, we were still conversing and communicating about faith.

The most poignant letter was in response to a question I raised about a rumour to the effect that he had left the Catholic Church, an assumption that had circulated among American Catholic intellectuals for a number of years. In a letter dated 1 August 1989, only two years before his death, Greene states:

> Your rumour is not quite correct. I usually go to Mass on a Sunday but sometimes I have too many people to see or too much work to do. I disagree with a good deal that the Pope has said and done but that doesn't mean that I have left the Church. I would call myself at the worst a Catholic agnostic.

In his last letter, dated 22 January 1991, Greene reiterates his dissatisfaction with, and disaffection for, the present Pope and Vatican. For me it is a painful letter, since it articulates the pangs of a deeply caring and loving son of the Church, one whose faith had been tested on earlier occasions when he had written *The Power and the Glory* (1940) and *The Heart of the Matter* (1948), novels that had raised serious moral and doctrinal questions concerning grace, free will and conscience, and moral rectitude. Had he pushed the traditional Catholic understanding of grace and redemption too far? Had he gone over the limit?

In *Ways of Escape* (1980) Greene recounts the difficulties *The Power and the Glory* had with the Vatican years after its publication:

> Some ten years after publication the Cardinal Archbishop of Westminster read me a letter from the Holy Office condemning my novel because it was "paradoxical" and dealt with "extraordinary circumstances".

Although the Catholic Church, through its Holy Office, had seriously considered condemning *The Power and the Glory*, a legal technicality kept it from appearing in the 1961 Index of Forbidden Books, a Vatican blacklisting of publications that was officially abolished on 14 June 1966. Greene claimed that the copyright was in the hands of his publisher, so there was little he could do to stop the publication of his book. Greene reveals a loyal appreciation for the Church's vigilance:

> The price of liberty, even within a Church, is eternal vigilance, but I wonder whether any of the totalitarian states, whether of the right or of the left, with which the Church of Rome is compared, would have treated me as gently when I refused to revise the book on the casuistical ground that the copyright was in the hands of my publishers. There was no public condemnation, and the affair was allowed to drop into that peaceful oblivion which the Church wisely reserves for unimportant issues.

If we are to understand Graham Thomas Greene's last crisis of faith, it is necessary we make certain distinctions. The first distinction concerns the general form of Catholic doctrine. The Church holds certain beliefs that are *de fide divina et definita*. These are dogma. They cannot be changed by anyone.

When reflecting on Graham Greene's last crisis of faith, we cannot suggest that he had rejected what the Church holds and has held *de fide divina et definita*. He never formally became an apostate. He never denounced the apostolic tradition of the Church, nor did he renounce the articles of faith that made him a Catholic in 1926. Doubt is not a sufficient cause to charge someone with apostasy. Greene's disagreements and objections centred on the manner in which a doctrinal issue was presented. Oddly, he suggested that "at worst he would consider himself a Catholic agnostic". What circumstances had led him in the last ten years to make such a statement?

Greene confesses to Marie-Françoise Allain in *The Other Man* that he believed in the impressive faith of the Mexican poor when he went there in 1938 to write about the persecution of the Church; and that miracles and magic are not something to be ignored. Of course, he makes it clear that much of his faith is linked to the plight of the underdog, a constant concern in his writing. He makes a personal distinction that is pivotal to his way of thinking:

> Faith is above belief. One can say that it's a gift of God, while belief is not. Belief is founded on reason. On the whole I keep my faith while enduring long periods of disbelief. At such moments I shrug my shoulders and tell myself I'm wrong—as though a brilliant mathematician had told me that my solution of an equation was wrong. My faith remains in the background, but it remains.

This distinction, so neatly drawn by Greene, can only be appreciated by an understanding of the philosopher Unamuno, whose existential writings permeate *Monsignor Quixote*. In a letter to me dated 15 February 1986, Greene answers my question about his readings of the controversial Spanish writer, whose books had been placed on the 1961 addition to the Index:

> ... About Unamuno whom I read of course in translation: I have read only *Our Lord Don Quixote, The Agony of Christianity, The Tragic Sense of Life, Ficciones* and *Novela.*

Greene had shown his penchant for Unamuno's paradoxical search for God in *Ways of Escape* when he cited him directly:

> Those who believe that they believe in God, but without passion in their hearts, without anguish of mind, without uncertainty, without doubt, without an element of despair even in their consolation, believe only in the God idea, not in God himself.

It is clear that for Greene a passionate relationship of the heart to

God, something he had witnessed among the Catholic poor while in Mexico, is crucial to faith. It may even be superior to those truths reached by reason and the conjectures of the mind. As Greene's biographer Norman Sherry points out in his first volume, in the author's 1925 convert classes with Fr Trollope in Nottingham there exists evidence of his mind seeking to understand faith, debating tenaciously the priest's arguments with a dogmatic atheism. However, the dictum *fides quaerens intellectum*—faith seeking understanding—seems to have evolved and changed by 1938, when Greene was searching for more visible, yet incomprehensible signposts of faith, religious expressions found and articulated especially by the poor in certain underdeveloped countries. From his observations of Roman Catholics as the downtrodden in anti-religious political societies, Greene was able to write about faith being above belief. It was from this circumstantial and historical context that Greene was also to appreciate in later years Latin America's movement toward a theology of liberation.

I am not suggesting that Greene became an intellectual ideologue of liberation theology through his readings, even though he writes in a postscript to a letter dated 4 January 1986:

PS The Cuban Ambassador in Panama gave me a copy of Fidel's liberation theology book in Spanish, but alas my Spanish is practically non-existent. I look forward very much to reading it in English.

Graham Greene's letters to me indicate a strong sympathy for the 'grassroots' piety inherent in the cultural expression of certain Latin American countries—which liberation theologians recognise as important in a world estranged from traditional ways of doing theology in Europe. For Greene, who travelled widely and whose concern centred always on the underdog wherever he went, the manifestations of faith were far more important that the specific beliefs articulated by an individual or a group of people.

Greene's letters to me indicate an avid interest in the revolutionary governments of Central America. In a letter dated 28 January 1983 he professes himself scandalised by the conditions set by the Vatican for Pope John Paul II's visit to Nicaragua:

> I doubt if the Pope's visit if it occurs will be of much value. He is only going to spend a day there and he will be sleeping in Costa Rica. He has also made it conditional on his visit that the two priests who are members of the Government should resign. This seems to me a rather scandalous intrusion by the head of one state into the internal affairs of another.

His letter to me of 18 March 1983 reveals his disappointment at two heads of state clashing, and also communicates his faith-in-action concept of Christianity for Central America:

> I wish that the Pope had not gone to Nicaragua. Daniel Ortega is a rather stupid man and it must have been tempting for him to speak out about the USA but he seems to have gone a bit too far. On the other hand I find it deplorable that the Pope had not got the charity to greet Father Cardenal who is a distinguished poet in a more friendly fashion. I don't think his visit to Nicaragua will have done his image any good there. This separation of faith and action which is what it amounts to is very unrealistic in Central America. It is impossible for a Catholic to remain on the side-lines.

A year later, on 8 October 1984, Greene tersely writes of his estrangement with John Paul II over liberation theology: "I find myself very much out of sympathy with the present Pope and his attack on liberation theology." On 8 November 1984 Greene expresses his satisfaction that the Jesuits are making a stand for liberation theology. And in his last letter to me, 22 January 1991, Greene seals our earthly decade of friendship by expressing his affection for the Society of Jesus when he writes: "Really, the only link I feel I have with the Catholic Church is with the Jesuit order."

There is no doubt that Greene's radical experience of the piety of the poor of Central America directed him to a different analysis of Christian action, one at variance with the institution he loved. Greene was inspired by what he had experienced over a long period of time as a journalist, novelist and essay-writer of Central American life, an inspiration that dates back to 1983 when he went to a Spanish-speaking country of the Americas for the first time. In Mexico he saw the strength of the Church in its courageous simplicity. This experience was to be confirmed in subsequent trips to other non-Spanish-speaking 'Third World' nations.

It is unfortunate that Greene was never invited as an experienced Catholic layman to advise the Vatican on how best to approach the real political and human situation in Central America, a complex situation where disappearance and martyrdom have become the daily bread of the poor and of those who lift their voices to protest the violent injustices perpetrated by self-serving political and economic alliances. Such a consultation never took place, and the institutional Church is poorer for having excluded Greene from this important dialogue. Whatever Greene's differences with the Vatican's understanding of liberation theology might have been, he was a Catholic to the end.

I was never to know what he thought of the 1990 US National Catholic News Service award-winning photograph, where two Jesuit seminarians kneel in prayer before a line of baton-carrying police at the US Federal Building in San Francisco, California, in order to protest against America's arms policy in El Salvador—a photograph I had sent him on 19 March. He died on 3 April in Switzerland. A model of true charity, he spent his last days encouraging his doctor not to feel bad because his medical expertise could do nothing more for him. Greene died with his good friend Fr Durán present. They prayed the rosary together, much as Don Quixote faces his dreams for a better world while Sancho weeps at the visions they had once shared intimately. For Fr Durán, a priest of many years, this was to be his first administration of the Sacrament of Extreme Unction, the Church's anointing for someone near death. Since he had been a university professor most of his career, this pastoral experience had never surfaced. Little had Durán realised that Greene had chosen him 27 years earlier with the confidence that God would not abandon him in his greatest hour of need. It was the end of a Catholic life passionately lived, and surrendered generously to a forgiving and merciful God.

NOTES

1. Hans Küng, controversial Swiss-born theologian, appointed official adviser during the 1962-1965 Vatican II reforms.

2. Miguel de Unamuno (1864-1936), Spanish philosopher. (For a fascinating account of Cervantes' influence on Unamuno and Graham Greene, see *Don Quixote's Delusions* by Miranda France, published in 2001.) Baron Friedrich von Hügel (1852-1925), Florentine theologian who, like Greene, thought God would always be "mysterious" to a degree. ("Religion can't be clear if it is worth anything," he wrote.) Frank Morrison, English journalist who set out to prove that Christ's resurrection was a myth; instead, in his book *Who Moved the Stone?*, written in 1930, he ended up defending the validity of the biblical record.

3. In a letter to *The Spectator* (30 July 1988), the atheist philosopher A. J. Ayer claimed to have suffered a "somewhat agonising but very astonishing experience" in hospital when his brain had continued to function during the four minutes of a heart arrest. "One might well fall back on the Christian doctrine of the resurrection of the body," the logical positivist begrudged.

4. FMLN: Frente Farabundo Martí para la Liberación Nacional.

5. Cardinal John Carmel Heenan (1905-1975), Roman Catholic Archbishop of Westminster known during World War II as the "Radio Priest" for his work with the BBC.

6. Archbishop Oscar Arnulfo Romero, "Prophet to the Americas", El Salvador priest assassinated in 1980 by the Salvadoran Army's anti-Communist forces.

7. Douglas Jerrold, Greene's immediate superior at Eyre & Spottiswoode, was a keen supporter of Franco. Despite his left-liberal Catholicism, the young Greene mixed with confessedly right-wing ideologues, and indeed from 1944 to 1948 worked as the editorial director of Eyre & Spottiswoode.

Appendix

OUR MAN IN TALLINN

GRAHAM GREENE'S CHANCE ENCOUNTER WITH A MODEL SPY

Tallinn Town Hall in the late 1920s when Vice-Consul Leslie
was first posted to the Baltic city.

"Estonians are nocturnal people and like to stay out all night.
However, it is generally not wise for His Majesty's Vice-
Consul to stay at cabaret restaurants after 2a.m., since
incidents sometimes occur."
(*Report on Personal Aspects of Life in Tallinn, Estonia.* Foreign
Office Circular Despatch, 28 April 1937.)

Graham Greene first visited the Estonian capital of Tallinn, some 250 miles west of St Petersburg, in the spring of 1934—"for no reason", he writes in his memoir *Ways of Escape*, "except escape to somewhere new". His fellow passenger on the flight from the Latvian capital of Riga was an ex-Anglican clergyman installed in Tallinn as a Foreign Office diplomat. The two men happened to be reading a Henry James novel in the same edition, and they struck up a conversation. They later spent "many happy hours" together in Tallinn, Greene records, "when I was not vainly seeking a brothel." The brothel had been recommended to the novelist by Baroness Budberg, a Russo-Baltic exile living in London and a mistress of H. G. Wells. (The brothel was famed for its antiquity and discretion.) Greene described his chance encounter as one of "the most pleasant" in his life.

Though Greene does not name the diplomat in *Ways of Escape*, Foreign Office files identify him as Peter Edmund James Leslie, appointed "His Majesty's Vice-Consul" in Tallinn on 12 February 1931. By any standards, Leslie's had been an exotic life. Prior to the First World War he served as Curate of the Church of the Ascension in East London, a turreted red-brick building down by Victoria Docks. The *Diocesan Yearbooks* for 1916 list "Reverend Leslie" as an Anglican army chaplain; at the war's end, however, he converted to Catholicism and joined a munitions firm (William Beardmore & Co) as a commercial salesman. Though not wealthy, he moved among patrician circles and had shares in a diamond mine in South Africa. One could imagine Leslie as a spy in an Eric Ambler novel and, it seems, he may have been a spy for the British government.

During the 1930s, Greene's brother Hugh was a journalist on the *Daily Telegraph* in Nazi Berlin; Greene called on him there en route to Tallinn in 1934. It is not known what the novelist's movements were in Hitler's Germany. On 4 May, however, Greene caught the midnight train from Berlin to Riga, and from there, on 12 May, he boarded a

Baroness Moura Budberg, whose recommendation of a Tallinn brothel came to nothing. (In 1965, after another disappointment, Graham Greene wrote to the Ukraine-born émigrée: "My dear Moura, You know that I love you very much, so you must forgive my telling you that you are being a bloody nuisance.")

small propeller plane to Tallinn: Vice-Consul Leslie was on the same flight. On arrival in Tallinn, Greene had tea with Leslie in the British Consulate at 17 Lai Street, and afterwards explored the Old City, or Vanalinn. Tallinn's medieval guildhalls, Russian Orthodox onion domes and twisting cobbled streets enchanted Greene. Baroness Budberg's directions, however, must have been inadequate as the novelist failed to find the bawdy house she had recommended. Later that evening Greene treated Leslie to a vodka-fuelled supper, before wandering back to the Golden Lion Hotel on Harju Street where he was staying. From his room he wrote a slightly tipsy letter to his wife Vivien, whom he nicknamed "Tiger" (Greene was her "Tyg"):

...I've been very lucky here. The train takes 10 hours to go the 100 miles from Riga, & as to fly only costs 25/-. I flew, a pretty flight along the edge of the Baltic. My luck was to share a taxi to the aerodrome with the Vice-Consul at Tallinn. I had tea with him when we arrived. A charming rather disappointed character, a Catholic who reads nothing but Henry James! I noticed when he unpacked his suitcase that he was carrying *The Ambassadors* with him. So we more or less fell into each other's arms...He has lived in Tallinn for 12 years with an interval when he was a commercial traveller in armaments. I gave him dinner tonight and tomorrow I'm having dinner with him. It's all amazingly cheap here. We had dinner, the two of us, 6 vodkas, a delicious hors d'oeuvres, 2 Vienna schnitzel with fried potatoes, & two glasses of tea. Total bill in one of the swell restaurants 3/6d....

Greene concluded: "Good night, dearest dearest heart, I'm going to bed early being sleepy after the vodkas", and signed off "Your Tyg". (The letter is now held in the Bodleian Library, Oxford.)

On his return to England that spring of 1934, Greene recommended the British diplomat to his journalist brother Hugh.

A mischievous Graham Greene in 1969 at the time of his
correspondence with Peter Leslie.

"Leslie, the nice Vice-Consul in Tallinn, wrote to ask me for a line of intro. to you. He'll be passing through Berlin while you are on holiday, so I suggested he might find you on the way back to Estonia." The evidence suggests, however, that the "nice" Leslie was Greene's first (and possibly inadvertent) contact with British Intelligence. Pre-war Tallinn was known to be a centre for espionage, infiltrated by White Russian intriguers intent on blocking Stalin's access to the city. By controlling the Estonian capital, Stalin could protect the Soviet Union against assault from Northwest Europe and command all Baltic territories. A Foreign Office clerk (name illegible) notes: "Leslie is one of the best representatives the SIS [the Secret Intelligence Service, or M16] have got in Eastern Europe."[1]

A film sketch conceived by Greene shortly after the war, "Nobody to Blame", concerns a British sales representative in Estonia ("Latesthia") for Singer Sewing Machines, who turns out to be an SIS spy. The film was never made as it poked fun at His Majesty's Secret Service; yet it contained the bare bones of what was to become "Our Man in Tallinn", later *Our Man in Havana* (1958). In 1988, anticipating my first visit to Tallinn,[2] I had written to Greene asking why he moved *Our Man in Havana* from Estonia in the 1930s to Cuba in the 1950s. Greene explained that a Secret Service comedy about a Hoover salesman who gets sucked up into espionage would be more credible in pre-Castro Havana, with its louche nightclubs, than in Soviet-occupied Tallinn. He concluded: "I already knew Cuba and my sympathies were with the Fidelistas in the mountains... One could hardly sympathise with the main character if he was to be involved in the Hitler war".

Of course Cuba could not be more different from Estonia. Yet Wormold, the Hoover salesman in Greene's Cuban "entertainment", is not unlike Leslie, the former munitions salesman in the Baltic.

While Wormold is said to be "uninterested in women", Leslie (in *Ways of Escape*) is actually "scared of women"; both men are old-fashioned merchant-scholars with a taste for vodka and books.

Peter Leslie's last posting was to Damascus, after which he retired to Norwich. His few surviving acquaintances there recalled a gentle, bookish man who collected stamps, was probably homosexual, and according to his travel agent wore double-breasted chalkstriped suits "almost green with age". Peter Leslie was popularly known as "Peter the Great". After Tallinn, Greene lost sight of Leslie and assumed he had disappeared in 1940, when Stalin invaded the Baltic outpost. In fact, when Soviet tanks rolled into Tallinn, Leslie had been made responsible for British interests in the city and afterwards fled to safety across the Gulf of Finland. (The British Consulate in Tallinn was subsequently turned into a Soviet blood transfusion centre.) Some thirty years later—out of the blue—Greene received a letter from him. It was written in the summer of 1969; Leslie had then just finished reading Greene's five essays on Henry James in *The Lost Childhood*, and these prompted a distant memory of the Baltic. Greene was sixty-four years old and about to publish his twenty-first novel, *Travels with My Aunt*. To his astonishment the ex-Vice-Consul wished to pass on his first editions of James. After a thirty-year silence, Leslie's seemed an extraordinarily generous offer. So began a delightful exchange of letters, five in all, over a period of eleven weeks, in the course of which Greene emerges as a sociable and considerate man, not at all the sternly introspective Catholic of his public image. Until now the Greene-Leslie correspondence has not been seen (it is held in the John J. Burns library, Boston College, Massachusetts).

Turret Cottage
66 Bethel Street
Norwich NOR 57E

19 August 1969

Dear Graham Greene,

A few months ago I read for the first time the volume of your essays, entitled *The Lost Childhood*. It brought back vividly to me the occasion of our encounter on a journey from Riga to Tallinn in the year 193-(?) Between the Rom Hotel, Riga, and the Airport we shared a taxi, and discovered that we were both devoted to the works of Henry James. I remember that you told me you had not read some of his works—notably *In the Cage*[3]—because you were saving them up for your old age. My reply was that I hoped to continue to enjoy them as old friends when I was old.

The object of this letter is to ask whether you would care to have a few first editions of the earlier works of Henry James. These are *A Passionate Pilgrim* (1875), *Transatlantic Sketches* (1875), *The American* (1877) and *French Poets and Novelists* (1878). I believe these are all first editions. I have also *The Portrait of a Lady* (1882) in one volume. It was originally published in two volumes. All these books were originally the property of Mrs Julia Revillon[4], a niece of James Whistler. She died in 1930, and I inherited them on the death of her son Joseph Whistler Revillon in 1955.

I have never taken any interest in first editions as such; but I would like to pass them on to someone who would appreciate them. I have also *Foreign Parts* (1883), *Portraits of Places* (1884) and *A Little Tour in France* (1885) in the original Tauchnitz editions. I would be very glad to send you all of these, if you would care to have them. I have now reached the advanced age of 86, and none of my surviving friends are readers of Henry James, so I thought I would write to you.

Yours sincerely,
Peter Leslie

P.S. I am on the point of leaving England for "cures" in Austria and Romania, but if you would reply with a nine-penny stamped letter, it would be forwarded, and I would send you the books on my return to Norwich early in October. P. L.

Three weeks later, on 3 September 1969, Greene replied from a flat on the Boulevard Malesherbes, Paris, where he was then living.

My dear Leslie,

How very nice to hear from you after all these years. I always remember the moment in the plane between Riga and Tallinn when we saw that we were reading a volume of Henry James in the same pocket Macmillan edition. Alas you were never able to find for me that brothel in Tallinn recommended by Moura Budberg which had been in the same family for 500 years.

It is very kind indeed of you to offer me those first editions. I have a number of James's firsts—including *In the Cage*, but not the ones you mention and I assure you that they will have a good home. I am living in France now but I wonder if you wouldn't mind sending them to my secretary, Miss Reid[5], at 9 Bow Street, London, W.C.2., as I move around so much. I wonder whether there is any chance of your looking in on me in Paris one day? I am astonished to hear that you are eighty-six. I am just reaching sixty-five and I never realised there were so many years between us.

Yours sincerely,

Graham Greene

P.S. As a poor return for the Henry James's I am asking my

Peter Leslie, retired Tallinn diplomat, at home in Norwich during the late 1960s, when he offered Graham Greene his first editions of Henry James.

secretary to send you the volume of *Collected Essays* which came out the other day.

Having returned from his "bronchial" mud-bath cures abroad, Leslie wrote to Greene on 16 October 1969:

Dear Graham Greene,

Thank you so much for your kind and friendly letter of 3rd Sept. It was forwarded to me in Austria. I am glad that you remember so vividly our encounter in the Baltic States. The one mistake you make is about the 500 year old brothel: it may once have been as Moura Budberg says, but in my time was merely a chemist's APOTHEKE in Radhaus Platz [Town Hall Square].[6]

I am delighted to know that you are living in the Boulevard Malesherbes. I like to imagine that it is in the same flat in which Chad Newsome[7] lived, and that you hang over the balcony, like Little Bilham, watching the stream of Paris life go by. It is good of you to suggest my looking in on you one day. I have avoided Paris of late years owing to the high cost of living, and have usually travelled to Austria, which I visit every year, via Harwich and the Hook, thus avoiding London too.

This year I have been further afield and after my chest cure at Bad Gleichenberg in Styria, flew on to Bucharest, where I stayed for the second time in the Clinic of Dr Anna Aslan[8], undergoing REJUVENATION treatment. I think it did me a lot of good, though I am still stiff in all the wrong places.

I have just written a line to your secretary, Miss Reid, advising her that six volumes of Henry James are being despatched to her by Mr Crowe, an Antiquarian Bookseller, who is my near neighbour.

I also acknowledged the receipt of your latest publication—*The Collected Essays*—for which I thank you very much. I shall value it greatly.

I note that you move around a lot. So do I. I reckon to be about six months in the year in Turret Cottage. I am most likely going for the winter to South Africa (where I have some money). But I have done nothing about it yet; and must now get busy. So I am unlikely to be in Paris this year.

If you ever come to Norwich, I can put you up in my little house, if I am in residence.

All good wishes,
Ever
Peter Leslie

Dr. Anna Aslan's controversial "rejuvenation" clinic in Bucharest offered to slow down and sometimes even reverse the ageing process. In his reply to Leslie of 18 October 1969, however, Greene questioned the Romanian doctor's claims to vivify the ex-diplomat. It was then common knowledge that Somerset Maugham had been left confused and senile after a Swiss doctor, Paul Niehans, injected him with lamb foetus cells. (The doctor had apparently complimented Maugham on his "lovely soft testicles".) Greene also took the opportunity to display his knowledge of the 1874-1914 French "Fantômas" detective series by Marcel Alain and Pierre Souvestre.

Dear Leslie,

Thank you for your letter. And I look forward enormously to receiving the books. I had quite forgotten that Chad Newsome lived in the Boulevard Malesherbes. I am sure that it would have been somewhere up this end near the Parc Monceau which is also the scene of many of the crimes of Fantômas.

I was in Romania a few years ago and heard much of Doctor Aslan, but after seeing what happened to Somerset Maugham at the hands of that Swiss quack I am reluctant to think of rejuvenation! However I am sure that Doctor Aslan is far better than the man [Dr Niehans] whose name I always Freudianly forget.

I have a brother Hugh who lives in East Anglia, and so who knows perhaps one day I shall be able to call on you in Norwich.

All good wishes,

Yours,
Graham

According to the Essex records, Peter Leslie died of "congestive heart failure" on 11 December 1971 in a private house in Colchester. Greene's final communication with him, dated 8 November 1969, was sent from Antibes:

Dear Leslie,

Your six James's arrived safely at Antibes and I have reconstructed my book-shelves to house them with proper dignity. They join ten other first editions so that now I have got a really good array. I can't tell you how grateful I am. A curious coincidence—soon after I got your letter about your James's I got a letter from an old friend of mine in America who was once my agent asking me whether I would like a signed photograph of James which had been given by him to her husband's father. I hope this flow of James material will continue to set in my direction.

I am off for ten days now to Anacapri, but I do hope that one day fate will take you in the direction of either Paris or Antibes.

What happy days I had in Estonia. I had quite a quarrel with my Communist guide once in Leningrad when I accused his leaders of colonialism. I would hate to go back [to Tallinn] now.

Yours ever,
Graham

Shortly before Christmas on 16 December 1971, Peter Leslie was cremated at St. Faith's Crematorium, Manor Road, Norwich. (Catholics were by then permitted to be cremated.) No lapidary commemoration or other engraving was made for him; instead his ashes were laid to rest in the Crematorium's "Rose Bed 69". The local *Eastern Daily Press* carried a brief death notice; Peter Edmund James Leslie was born in Belfast in 1883 to a chemist father. He had no children and had never married. A Requiem Mass was held for him in Norwich at St. John the Baptist Roman Catholic Church. *If you ever come to Norwich, I can put you up in my little house.* Sadly Greene never was reunited with the Tallinn ex-Vice Consul. Peter Leslie had died at the age of eighty-eight before the novelist could visit him. Graham Greene himself died twenty years later—in 1991, six months short of his eighty-seventh birthday.

Ian Thomson
Tallinn, 2006

NOTES

1. London Public Records dossier FO 369/1757.
2. *The Independent* Magazine had sent me there to explore my Baltic roots; my mother had grown up in formerly Czarist Tallinn in the 1930s when Greene visited.
3. *In the Cage* is a late short novel by Henry James about a telegraph operator who deduces an adultery from the telegrams she reads.
4. Julia Revillon was the half-Russian niece of the American artist James Whistler. Her civil engineer son Joseph was in contact with a number of Whistler's associates and admirers, among them Peter Leslie.
5. Josephine Reid reportedly instilled fear in some people—even in Greene. "Miss R[eid] goes round with the face of a corpse," Greene wrote to his French lover Yvonne Cloetta in 1965.
6. The chemist's is still standing in Raekoja Plats (as the square is known in Estonian). For ten generations since 1585 it had been owned by the same Hungarian family.
7. Chad Newsome is a character in Henry James' novel *The Ambassadors*.
8. Nadia Comaneci, the Romanian Olympic gold medallist, currently endorses Dr Aslan's "GeroVital" skin care products.

Index